NK1650 .S55 1988

Institute for Worship Studies - Florida

CYCLE C
DECORATING
For Sundays & Holy Days

FROM THE LIBRARY OF
THE INSTITUTE FOR
WORSHIP STUDIES
FLORIDA CAMPUS

*THEMES
HOMILY SUGGESTIONS
ACTIVITIES*

CYCLE C
DECORATING
For Sundays & Holy Days

Bernadette McCarver Snyder & Hazelmai McCarver Terry

FROM THE LIBRARY OF
THE INSTITUTE FOR
WORSHIP STUDIES
FLORIDA CAMPUS

TWENTY-THIRD PUBLICATIONS
Mystic, Connecticut

Twenty-Third Publications
185 Willow Street
P.O. Box 180
Mystic, CT 06355
(203) 536-2611

©1988 Bernadette McCarver Snyder and Hazelmai McCarver Terry. All rights reserved. No part of this publication may be reproduced in any manner without prior written permission of the publisher.

ISBN 0-89622-372-8
Library of Congress Catalog Card Number 88-72014

Edited by Mary Carol Kendzia
Interior design by John G. van Bemmel
Cover design by Kathy Michalove

All photos (except those on pages 12, 90, 94, 116, 135) are by Togue Uchida Studio, Nashville, Tennessee.

We dedicate this book to our mother, Hazel Davids McCarver, who taught us that every day can be a celebration if you look through the lens of faith to find opportunity in the ordinary and commitment in the commonplace.

We also dedicate it to Liturgy Committees everywhere—in the hope that our small suggestions will lead them to new avenues of opportunity and commitment.

Contents

Introduction	11
First Sunday of Advent	16
Second Sunday of Advent	18
Third Sunday of Advent	20
Fourth Sunday of Advent	22
Christmas	24
Holy Family Sunday	26
Octave of Christmas solemnity of mary	28
Epiphany	30
Baptism of the Lord	32
Second Sunday in Ordinary Time	34
Third Sunday in Ordinary Time	36
Fourth Sunday in Ordinary Time	38
Fifth Sunday in Ordinary Time	40
First Sunday of Lent	42
Second Sunday of Lent	46
Third Sunday of Lent	48
Fourth Sunday of Lent	50
Fifth Sunday of Lent	52
Passion Sunday (palm sunday)	54
Holy Thursday	56
Good Friday	56

Holy Saturday	57
Easter Sunday	58
Second Sunday of Easter	60
Third Sunday of Easter	62
Fourth Sunday of Easter	64
Fifth Sunday of Easter	66
Sixth Sunday of Easter	68
Seventh Sunday of Easter	70
Pentecost Sunday	72
Trinity Sunday	74
The Body and Blood of Christ	76
Sixth Sunday in Ordinary Time	78
Seventh Sunday in Ordinary Time	80
Eighth Sunday in Ordinary Time	82
Ninth Sunday in Ordinary Time	84
Tenth Sunday in Ordinary Time	86
Eleventh Sunday in Ordinary Time	88
Twelfth Sunday in Ordinary Time	90
Thirteenth Sunday in Ordinary Time	92
Fourteenth Sunday in Ordinary Time	94
Fifteenth Sunday in Ordinary Time	96
Sixteenth Sunday in Ordinary Time	98

SEVENTEENTH SUNDAY IN ORDINARY TIME	100
EIGHTEENTH SUNDAY IN ORDINARY TIME	102
NINETEENTH SUNDAY IN ORDINARY TIME	104
TWENTIETH SUNDAY IN ORDINARY TIME	106
TWENTY-FIRST SUNDAY IN ORDINARY TIME	108
TWENTY-SECOND SUNDAY IN ORDINARY TIME	110
TWENTY-THIRD SUNDAY IN ORDINARY TIME	112
TWENTY-FOURTH SUNDAY IN ORDINARY TIME	114
TWENTY-FIFTH SUNDAY IN ORDINARY TIME	116
TWENTY-SIXTH SUNDAY IN ORDINARY TIME	118
TWENTY-SEVENTH SUNDAY IN ORDINARY TIME	120
TWENTY-EIGHTH SUNDAY IN ORDINARY TIME	122
TWENTY-NINTH SUNDAY IN ORDINARY TIME	124
THIRTIETH SUNDAY IN ORDINARY TIME	126
THIRTY-FIRST SUNDAY IN ORDINARY TIME	128
THIRTY-SECOND SUNDAY IN ORDINARY TIME	130
THIRTY-THIRD SUNDAY IN ORDINARY TIME	132
CHRIST THE KING	134

CYCLE C
DECORATING
For Sundays & Holy Days

Introduction

This is a book about possibilities, a book about reunions, celebrations, and friends.

Have you ever been to a family reunion? Or an anniversary celebration? Or a get-together with good friends? Sure you have! You go to one every weekend. Every Sunday at Mass we gather together for a reunion with our neighborhood family of God, a get-together with good friends, an anniversary celebration remembering the Last Supper. We break bread together, sing together, rejoice, and thank God together. For a celebration this special, do we really need to add anything? Do we need decorations?

Let's consider the possibilities.

For many years, Mass was always celebrated with white altar cloths, formal flower arrangements, and candles burning in golden candle holders. The atmosphere this created was solemn, impressive, and beautiful, and many of us loved it.

But some people felt so awe-struck by the overall atmosphere that for them God seemed *too* far away, *too* unapproachable. They felt this formality did not reflect the feeling of that evening when Jesus got together with his friends, broke bread, and said, "This is my body."

Liturgy today, like modern life, offers an ever-widening scope of possibilities. Just as prayer has many forms—from formal, memorized words or rituals, to spontaneous conversation—liturgy, too, can range from an hour-long, elaborate concelebration in a crowded cathedral to a brief, early morning Mass in a small chapel with only a few people present.

In keeping with this diversity, altar decorations can also range from the familiar starched cloths and polished candlesticks, to burlap and baskets of polished apples, or sailcloth and seashells, or astroturf and daisies.

These decorations should never detract nor draw attention from the Mass. Instead, they should always point toward and draw attention to the significance of the feast, the readings of the day, and the miracle of the eucharist.

Decorations should not be memorable in or of themselves. Rather, they should present a "memory trigger" for the assembly to take home with them, so that during the week they can recall the message of the Sunday or feast day readings, and find a way to apply that message to their daily lives.

A few years ago, we wrote a book entitled *Decorations for 44 Parish Celebrations,* in which we outlined ways to "enhance liturgy tastefully and simply." Since then, we have been asked, "When are you going to do a follow-up with more decoration ideas?" This book answers that question.

As I mentioned at the beginning, this is a book of possibilities. It is not an answer book. We are only presenting decorations that *could* be used. Some are ideas that we have used in our respective parishes; some are decorations we've seen used in various parishes when visiting or on vacation. It is our hope that these suggestions will serve as stepping-stones that lead you to plan decorations uniquely appropriate for your own parish.

One of the most special gifts that God has given us is variety—endless possibilities in every day, in every person, around every corner. In God's many-splendored world, you never know what's going to happen next. If 10 people read the same Scripture passage, they might easily get 10 different messages. If 100 people attend Mass, each might have a different reaction or response to God's call. God does not limit us. We only limit ourselves.

So, when planning your decorations, think "What if...?" "How about...?" "Why not...?" Look around at the variety, the imagination, the creativity in God's world. Incorporate these into your parish celebrations. For what better way to give thanks for this diversity and splendor than by using it to praise God in prayer and in liturgy?

Although these decorations and celebrations are designed primarily for Sunday Mass, they could easily be adapted for use in schools, family gatherings, or other liturgical celebrations outside the church setting.

How to Use This Book
Each Sunday or feast day is set up in simple sections:

Inspiration—A brief selection from the readings of the day that suggest a decoration theme. In reflecting on the readings, you may find a passage that will suggest a totally different decoration to you.

Decoration and Additions—Possibilities for carrying out the theme, and extras that could be used in the church other than near the altar.

Celebration—An activity that can be planned to tie in with the theme of the day.

Reflection—A thought that could be read before Mass, or printed (in whole or part) in the bulletin, or used as a springboard for the homily.

• We suggest that these decorations *not* be placed on the altar itself. Instead, you should devise some way to place them in front of and below the main altar—possibly on a small, low table.

• Depending on the architecture of your church, there are times when you might want to use a large oversize banner or piece of art behind the altar, or small banners hanging from the ceiling. You might also want to try decorations above or between the windows, or a banner or poster at the back of church which can be seen only as the parishioners are leaving.

• You can construct a large mobile to hang from the ceiling above the altar or two smaller mobiles to hang on each side. Once you have built these and found a way to hang them, it would be easy to vary the decoration by hanging different designs from the mobile for each season.

• You might consider having a banner or poster in the vestibule of the church that announces the theme of the particular Sunday as parishioners arrive each Sunday. This space can also be creatively used to announce any special celebration that might be held after Mass in conjunction with the liturgy of the day.

• The liturgy committee in your parish may not have enough time or enough workers to plan special decorations for every weekend. If this is the case, choose whichever Sundays would be most appropriate for your parish. On each non-decoration Sunday, you can announce that this is a "meditation Sunday." Parishioners are then asked to meditate on the readings and think what decoration they might have used if they had been on the liturgy committee. (Perhaps some will share their ideas with you, and you will not only discover new decoration possibilities but perhaps even find parishioners who would be valuable additions to the liturgy committee!)

• Since this book is designed to be used on Sundays in any cycle C year, it does not include decorations for seasonal days like Mother's Day, Memorial Day, or Labor Day. You can find decorations for this type of holiday in our other book, *Decorations for 44 Parish Celebrations* (Mystic, Connecticut: Twenty-Third Publications, 1983).

First Sunday of Advent

Jeremiah 33: 14-16
Thessalonians 3: 12—4:2
Luke 21: 25-28, 34-36

In those days, in that time, I will raise up for David a just shoot; he shall do what is right and just in the land.

Decoration

Today the focal point will of course be the Advent wreath, now available in a variety of styles from the traditional to an oversized one that can be suspended from the ceiling. Consider a simple addition—a purple felt background with three terra cotta or clay flower pots. Fill the first pot with only dirt, the second with a bulb just beginning to sprout, the third with a bulb sprouting a tall shoot. (Narcissus bulbs should be available at this time of the year. If not, you can make "shoots" of green construction paper).

Addition—A banner with the design of a sprouting bulb and the words, "He shall do what is right and just in the land...." Or a banner with a twisting path leading into the distance, and the words, "Your ways, O Lord, make known to me." Or a mobile with a design of Advent candles.

Celebration

In the vestibule, place a very large dead branch, securely planted in a pot of dirt. Nearby, have wicker baskets filled with green construction paper "shoots" and short strips of green ribbon, along with some pencils or pens. Ask parishioners to consider what they could do during Advent to be a "just shoot."

Invite them to stop after Mass to take one of the green shoots, write a few words on it to indicate their Advent promise and then attach it to the tree with a ribbon. Keep this tree, with its budding shoots, on display during Advent as a reminder of this promise Sunday. If a branch is not available, you can make a large drawing of a bare-branched tree and attach the shoots with pins.)

Reflection

Advent is a time of waiting. Most people today are familiar with waiting. We wait in checkout lines at the supermarket, in traffic jams, at the doctor's office, for the next paycheck. We wait for the children to grow up—for the babies to learn to walk, the toddlers to learn to talk, and the teenagers to come home with the car.

On this first Sunday of Advent, the first reading says, "I will raise up for David a just shoot." The altar decorations remind us that perhaps God, too, is waiting, waiting for us to bud forth as a just shoot, to grow in spirituality, to walk in the paths of the Lord, to talk of God's goodness and listen to the teachings of Scripture.

Consider what you could do this Advent to start to become a "just shoot"; perhaps a daily prayer, a penance, or a charitable act. After Mass, you'll find a basket of green "shoots" in the vestibule. Take one and write on it a few words that symbolize your promise. Then add it to our Advent parish promise tree.

Second Sunday of Advent

Baruch 5: 1-9
Philippians 1: 4-6, 8-11
Luke 3: 1-6

My prayer is that your love may more and more abound...so that...you may learn to value the things that really matter....

Decoration

Place a Christmas "giving" tree in the sanctuary or vestibule. Instead of the usual ornaments or lights, tie on Christmas pictures cut from last year's Christmas cards or simple Christmas designs (stars, candles, wreaths) pasted on red and white construction paper. (Have these made ahead of time by the children, or another parish group.) On the back of each ornament write the name of one item that can be given to a poor family for Christmas.

Addition—Two banners: "Learn to value the things that really matter" and "Make ready the way of the Lord...."

Celebration

Contact a poor parish and ask them to give you a list of items that families there may need. They could give you specific items and sizes for a particular family—woman's sweater, size 16; boy's corduroy pants, size 10. Or they could give you general items which are needed; blankets, warm mittens, canned hams, or a toy for a pre-schooler. The size of your parish will determine how many of these items you can promise to collect.

Write the name of an item on one of the ornaments before you tie it on the tree. Then ask parishioners to take an ornament from the tree and purchase the gift indicated. You will need a small committee to pack the presents and deliver them to the poor parish before Christmas. (Remember someone might take an ornament and then not be able to bring the requested gift because of a family emergency, sickness, etc. Therefore, you should have some parish funds available to buy a few extra gifts at the last minute in order to deliver all the gifts you promised.)

Reflection

In the midst of Christmas shopping and wrapping, buying and charging, do we really believe it is more blessed to give than to receive? No matter how strained your budget may be this month, there are many people in your city who are much less fortunate. They may have no Christmas dinner, no gifts, no toys for the children. Since these people are members of our own family—our family of God—we invite you to remember them with one small Christmas gift this year.

The tree in our sacristy today is a "giving tree." On the back of each ornament is a request for one gift for a poor family. We ask you to take an ornament, purchase the gift requested, gift-wrap it, put a label on the outside to indicate what the package contains, and put it under the tree. On the last Sunday before Christmas, we'll deliver these gifts to ____ parish to be given to poor families.

Today's second reading asks us to "learn to value the things that really matter." We hope the giving tree will remind us all that in this blessed season, Christian charity and love of neighbor are what really matter.

Third Sunday of Advent

Zephaniah 3: 14-18
Philippians 4: 4-7
Luke 3: 10-18

The Lord himself is near. Dismiss all anxiety from your minds. Present your needs to God in every form of prayer and in petitions full of gratitude. Then God's own peace...will stand guard over your hearts and minds.

Decoration

You will want the Advent wreath and the giving tree to be the focus today, so you will not need to use any other decorations. (Note: When you remove the giving tree gifts on the last Sunday of Advent, you can redecorate this tree to use as part of the Christmas display.)

Addition—Banner with the words, "The Lord himself is near. Dismiss all anxiety from your minds." You can also use the design of the four Advent candles or the Advent wreath on the banner.

Celebration

Your giving tree may already have a lot of gifts under it, since parishioners may have brought them in during the week. But as an extra reminder to those who haven't shopped yet, you could arrange ahead of time to have a family or a few school children come up at the Offertory with their gifts.

Reflection

In this busy "countdown to Christmas" time, the second reading tells us, "The Lord himself is near. Dismiss all anxiety from your minds." It isn't easy to dismiss anxiety when you're in a hurry; this reading offers us the opportunity to really think about the words "dismiss anxiety." Are you so caught up in Christmas preparations that you haven't had time to really think about Advent? Did you promise to do something special during Advent and then get too busy to follow through? Dismiss anxiety. Instead of feeling guilty and troubled about what you "meant to do," use these last days of Advent to say one small quiet prayer each day so that, as the reading tells us "God's own peace...can stand guard over your heart and mind."

Today the school children (the _____ family) bring up gifts in the offertory procession representing the gifts we as a parish will be giving to _____ parish to make Christmas brighter for their parishioners. If you plan to contribute to the giving tree, please remember to bring your gift, wrapped and labeled, and put it under the tree before next Sunday so that we can deliver the gifts before Christmas.

Fourth Sunday of Advent

Micah 5: 1-4
Hebrews 10: 5-10
Luke 1: 39-45

Lord, make us turn to you, let us see your face and we shall be saved.

Decoration

In addition to the Advent wreath and giving tree, use a small table with a white cloth as the background for a display of Christmas cards, interspersed with greenery. Or use one large or several small wicker baskets stuffed with cards and addressed envelopes. Tie Christmas bows on the basket handles.

Addition—Banner with the design of a pen or pencil and the words "Dear Jesus..." or "All I want for Christmas is...."

Celebration

Plan to have a parish "quiet hour" this afternoon, or whatever time would be most convenient for your parish. For the quiet hour, fill the altar with greenery and many lighted vigil lights. Do not have any music or planned activity; just have the church open so that people can drop in for a quiet visit and "turn to the Lord."

Reflection

Our decoration of Christmas cards reminds us of the fact that this is the time of year when most of us send cards and letters to friends, relatives, and acquaintances. If there are children in your home, maybe they sent a letter to Santa. But is there someone you forgot? Our responsorial psalm today says, "Lord, make us turn to you." In this last week before Christmas, consider writing a Christmas card to Jesus. Tell him what you really want for Christmas this year—a new job, a new outlook on life, health, patience, acceptance, a spirit of joy.

To help you spend some time thinking this over, we will have a quiet hour this afternoon. The church will be open from 3 P.M. to 4 P.M. so that you can drop by, sit quietly, and "turn to the Lord." Think about what gift you would really like to get this Christmas. Ask for the one gift that could make your life more Christ-like.

CHRISTMAS
Midnight Mass

Isaiah 9: 1-6
Titus 2: 11-14
Luke 2: 1-14

(Readings will vary with other Masses of the day but this decoration would still be appropriate as all the readings mention light and darkness.)

The people who walked in darkness have seen a great light; upon those who dwelt in the land of gloom a light has shone.

Decoration

Place the Nativity scene in front of the altar. For the background, use several yards of white nylon net or tulle mingled with strings of miniature white Christmas lights. You might want to include a few strings of blinking lights, but only the tiny white ones, like sparkling stars. To the side you can add one or more Christmas trees, again decorated with tiny white lights. Windows can have Christmas wreaths or garlands, also decorated with the little white lights but with the addition of red velvet bows.

Addition—Large horizontal banner behind the altar with the words, "The people who walked in darkness have seen a great light...for a child is born to us, a son is given us...his dominion is vast and forever peaceful."

Celebration

If possible, have the church in semi-darkness, lit mostly by candles and the glittering lights in the decorations. Invite everyone to bring a small bell to Mass. As the Offertory song is sung (possibly "Joy to the World"), choir members can start ringing bells as a signal for all to join in with their bells. As the bells and song ring out, turn on the lights one at a time, so that by the end of the song the church is fully lighted.

Reflection

Tonight (today) we rejoice in our Lord's birth, the coming of the Light of the World. The people who waited in darkness for a savior saw a great light and found abundant joy, and each year we follow them in rejoicing. We tremble, insecure humans afraid of the dark. To us, darkness often symbolizes loneliness, evil, and uncertainty, even ignorance.

The Christmas readings and psalms speak of light; those "who walked in darkness have seen a great light," "a light will shine on us this day," "may the light of faith shine in our words and actions." As we celebrate this Christmas, let us pray that we Christians who have been filled with the light of faith will go forth into the new year and spread light on the ignorance and fear of the world. Let us pray that we will no longer be afraid of the dark, but filled with the Light of the World.

Holy Family Sunday

Sirach 3: 2-6, 12-14
Colossians 3: 12-21
Luke 2: 41-52

Bear with one another; forgive whatever grievances you have against one another. Forgive as the Lord has forgiven you.

Decoration

Since all the Christmas decorations will still be in place, the crib scene is certainly the perfect focus for Holy Family Sunday.

Addition—If they would not distract from the Christmas decorations, you could add two banners, possibly hung in front of the lecterns or in the back of church. One would be lettered, "Forgive whatever grievances you have against one another." The second one would have the words, "Forgive as the Lord has forgiven you."

Celebration

Before the second reading, mention the significance of the feast of the Holy Family. Suggest that families might like to join hands as they listen to this second reading.

Reflection

Today, as we celebrate Holy Family Sunday, no altar decoration could be more appropriate than the Nativity scene, which focuses on the three people who are the perfect role models for us all. We sometimes think of Jesus, Mary, and Joseph as only figures on a holy card. But they were real people who faced the everyday problems, irritations, and frustrations that all families do. They could understand how difficult it sometimes is to accept the words of today's second reading: "Forgive whatever grievances you have against one another...Christ's peace must reign in your hearts...dedicate yourself to thankfulness." This Christmas season is the perfect time to ask the Holy Family to help you forgive, find peace, and be thankful for whatever you have, even though it might not be "just what you always wanted."

OCTAVE OF CHRISTMAS
SOLEMNITY OF MARY

Numbers 6: 22-27
Galatians 4: 4-7
Luke 2: 16-21

Mary treasured all these things and reflected on them in her heart.

Decoration
If your church has a statue of Mary, you could put a bright blue drape behind the statue to highlight it on this special day. Add a bank of blue vigil lights or blue candles of various heights in front of the statue. You could center a small treasure chest among the burning candles.

Addition—A mobile made of strips of blue felt as a background for white felt silhouettes of Mary in different poses—standing, seated, holding the Christ Child. Or you could use the strips as a series of banners suspended from the ceiling, coming down the side aisles. Or use a simple blue and white banner with the words, "Hail Mary, full of grace."

Celebration
Purchase or collect a large number of small glass containers, for example, baby food jars. Fill these with holy water and have them on a table in the vestibule. Invite each family to take some holy water home for the New Year.

Reflection
Today, as we celebrate the Solemnity of Mary, Mother of God, the Gospel notes that "Mary treasured all these things and reflected on them in her heart," just as all mothers treasure family memories, and all fathers and children the same. Today we begin a New Year and welcome a new start, a new beginning, a new chance to make things better in our homes and in our lives.

In celebration of this Marian feast and the new year, we

invite you to stop by the vestibule and take along a small container of holy water. When you get home, you can use the holy water to make a cross on the forehead of each family member. Or sprinkle it in each room of your home as you say a prayer asking for help in cleansing the hearts of your family of all bitterness and resentment. Keep the holy water on hand and use it frequently in the new year to make the sign of the cross, blessing yourself and your family.

Perhaps this New Year's Day would also be a good time to get out the family album and to look through it together, sharing the memories it stirs and—as Mary did—treasuring these things and reflecting on them in your heart.

Epiphany

Isaiah 60: 1-6
Ephesians 3: 2-3. 5-6
Matthew 2: 1-12

We observed his star at its rising and have come to pay him homage.

Decoration
Make silver stars of various sizes from foil or silver wrapping paper, or by painting cardboard with silver paint. Attach these to threads and suspend them from the ceiling over the crib scene.

Addition—A banner using a design of three crowns, three camels or three gifts, and the words "We have come to pay him homage." Ask three people (three ushers, or a family of three, or three small children) to bring up three gifts and place them by the Nativity scene. They could come down the aisle with the entrance procession or at the presentation of the gifts.

One gift could be a gold jewelry box, or a tangle of gold costume jewelry piled on a gold tray, or the treasure box used in the Marian display last Sunday. Another could be an incense burner, or a fancy container such as the kind that usually holds bath salts. The third, for myrrh, could be a large, fancy perfume bottle.

Celebration
Since this will be the last Sunday for the Christmas decorations, you might invite everyone to the parish hall for a "Christmas Coffee/Rehash." If you feel ambitious, serve corned beef hash with poached eggs. Otherwise, just serve star-shaped cookies with coffee. Encourage everyone to share funny stories that happened during the Christmas holidays.

Reflection
Today we celebrate the feast of Epiphany, a word that means "manifest." Our star decorations remind us of the

time when three Wise Men followed a star to discover the appearance, the manifestation, of God among men. Recall today how God has made himself manifest in your life. How does *your* life make God manifest to others? Are you an Epiphany? Does God appear on earth to others through you?

Baptism of the Lord

Isaiah 42: 1-4, 6-7
Acts 10: 34-38
Luke 3: 15-16, 21-22

You are my beloved son. On you my favor rests.

Decoration
Make an arrangement of all different sizes and shapes of mirrors—a lady's compact mirror, hand mirror, wall mirror, round, square, framed or not, fancy or plain. You might want to intersperse these with large pieces of aluminum foil, slightly crushed or twisted to increase the brilliance of the mirrors and the idea of reflection.
Addition—Two banners, possibly with small mirrors or silver sequins glued on, one worded "Who am I?" the other worded "What is my calling?"

Celebration
If there is an upcoming baptism in the parish, either of a baby or a convert, this would be a good day to have a baptism during Mass. If the family of the newly-baptized is agreeable, you could even invite all present to the church basement for a "welcome to the church" party, and serve something simple, like punch and pretzels.

Reflection
Have you ever been totally surprised by discovering some unsuspected aspect or interest of a good friend, or maybe even of your husband or wife? Just when you thought you knew everything there was to know about them, they reveal to you a secret desire to be a matador, or they go to school to study Chinese, or begin to paint pictures when they never before had shown any interest in art.
In Scripture, we see Jesus constantly revealing himself in new ways. In today's first reading the prophet speaks of "my servant...with whom I am well pleased," and we think of

Jesus as a servant to his people. In the second reading we hear Peter speaking of "the good news of peace as proclaimed by Jesus Christ," and we think of Jesus as a proclaimer, a preacher. And then in the Gospel, Jesus is baptized, and a voice from heaven is heard to say, "You are my beloved son," and we see Jesus as the son of God, our savior.

Today's altar decoration of mirrors reminds us of the many reflections of Jesus, of how little we still know of him and how much more we have to learn. It also reminds us to look more closely at ourselves and ask, "Who am I? What is my calling? What must I do with my life so that some day God will look at me and see a servant in whom God is well pleased?"

Second Sunday in Ordinary Time

Isaiah 62: 1-5
1 Corinthians 12: 4-11
John 2: 1-12

Jesus performed this first of his signs at Cana in Galilee and his disciples believed in him.

Decoration

Make a display of framed wedding pictures from parish families and your own. Old ones will be especially interesting, or photos of bridal couples the parishioners might recognize. Intersperse with poufs of white net and center with two clear glass goblets, one filled with water, the other with wine. If you can't assemble a collection of photos, you could use one wedding album opened at a photograph of the bridal party. Another alternative would be to use only the goblets of wine and water with a lot of white net and sprays of real or artificial white flowers.

Addition—Mobile with designs that resemble water jars or chalices. Banner with the water jar design and the words, "Thus did he reveal his glory...."

Celebration
Several weeks ahead, plan to have a celebration on this day honoring all couples in the parish who have been married twenty-five years or longer. Announce it in the bulletin and ask couples to make reservations. Either have a communion breakfast or a catered dinner in the evening. Make it a festive, happy event that can become an annual celebration honoring the sacrament of matrimony. You could use some of the photographs from the altar decoration to decorate the tables for the breakfast or dinner, again using the net and/or flowers.

Reflection
Today's Gospel tells us that Jesus bowed to his mother's wishes and performed the first of his miracles at the wedding feast at Cana. "Thus did he reveal his glory...." The church has always honored the marriage bond and the holy sacrament of matrimony. And so, as we recall Cana today, this seems an appropriate time for our own parish to celebrate the commitment of marriage. To do this, we are honoring all parishioners who have been married twenty-five years or longer at a special Communion breakfast (dinner) this morning (evening). In this coming week, we also ask all parishioners to join in praying for those who may be experiencing marriage problems, so that "what God has joined together shall not be put asunder."

Third Sunday in Ordinary Time

Nehemiah 3: 2-4, 5-6, 8-10
1 Corinthians 12: 12-30 or 12: 12-14, 27
Luke 1: 1-4; 4: 14-21

The body is one and has many members, but all the members, many though they are, are one body; and so it is with Christ.

Decoration
Why not use puzzles for today's decoration? There are many parts that all combine to make one picture or design. You might find a beautiful wooden puzzle or jigsaw puzzle that forms a picture of the world, or a group of people, or some such appropriate design. If you use several puzzles, you could put one together, have another with a few pieces missing, or a basket full of unassembled pieces. You could also add a loaf of sliced bread or something else that illustrates "many parts that make one." As usual, you'll probably want to add a bit of greenery to fill out the arrangement.

Addition—Mobile made of "body parts," i.e., face, shirt, jeans, hands, and feet (or tennis shoes). Or a mobile made of several people dressed in ethnic clothing possibly cut from a child's book. Or make two banners, one lettered "...many members, one body...," the other lettered, "...so it is with Christ."

Celebration
Ask one member from each of several parish organizations—parish council, catechists, choir member, usher, etc.—to bring up the gifts. If you have a very "crafty" parish, this would be a good time to have a sale of parish-made crafts after one or more Masses, to show the diversity of talents in your faith community. If you need extra volunteers for parish activities, use today to give out sign-up sheets.

Reflection

If you're wondering why we have puzzles as today's decoration, it is to emphasize today's second reading which tells us, "...all the members, many though they are, are one body...and so it is with Christ." We are all different, all separate and yet all one, part of the Mystical Body. Members of various parish organizations will bring up the gifts today to again emphasize the diversity in unity. We all have different talents, different interests and different lives, yet it is the Christian way to work together, to help and inspire each other. In Paul's letter to the Corinthians he tells us today that "all of us, whether Jew or Greek, slave or free, were baptized into one body."

Fourth Sunday in Ordinary Time

Jeremiah 1: 4-5, 17-1
1 Corinthians 12: 31-13, 13 or 13: 4-13
Luke 4: 21-30

Before I formed you in the womb I knew you, before you were born I dedicated you.

Decoration

Today use only a baby's crib or a doll's cradle, set in front of the altar. Put in it a lacy coverlet or baby blanket. Lay on that one red rose. (Since real roses are so fragile, it might be best to use an artificial one.)

Addition—Use a banner with a pro-life design, for example, a baby's hands, and the words, "Before I formed you in the womb I knew you...." Another banner, with the design of a rose, could be lettered, "Before you were born, I dedicated you...."

Celebration

Since this Sunday falls near the anniversary of the Supreme Court decision to legalize abortion—January 22—this would be an appropriate time to have a "Pro-Life Shower." Two weeks prior to this Sunday, announce this in the bulletin and ask parishioners to bring any kind of baby clothes and miscellaneous items to be donated to a local agency that helps unwed mothers. At the Offertory, you could ask members of a pro-life group to bring up the donated items and place them by the crib. Or you could invite the whole congregation to bring up their gifts at this time. You might also have some blank envelopes in the pews so if anyone forgot to bring a gift, they could put cash in the envelope and bring it up. If the donations are not brought up at the Offertory, you can have some tables or baskets in the vestibule where parishioners can leave their gifts.

Reflection

This month we observe (last month we observed) the anniversary of the Supreme Court decision to legalize abortion on January 22. Today's first reading presents the Catholic pro-life position in the best possible words: "Before I formed you in the womb, I knew you...before you were born I dedicated you." We bring gifts today at the Offertory to help women who have chosen not to abort their unborn babies. Our altar decoration of an empty baby crib reminds us to respect all human life, and to renew our commitment to uphold its sacredness.

Fifth Sunday in Ordinary Time

Isaiah 6: 1-2, 3-8
1 Corinthians 15: 1-11 or 15: 3-8, 11
Luke 5: 1-11

...he said to Simon, "Put out into deep water and lower your nets for a catch." Simon answered, "Master, we have been hard at it all night long and have caught nothing; but if you say so, I will lower the nets."

Decoration

Large piece of fishnet as background drape, fishing pole, creel, lures, other fishing gear. Possibly add a bowl of live goldfish, trailing greenery such as seaweed, a canoe paddle, an antique-looking ship, or large, craggy rocks.

Addition—Banner with fish design and the words, "Do not be afraid. From now on you will be catching people." Banner with boat design and the words, "They brought their boats to land, left everything, and became his followers." Mobile with various sizes and types of fish.

Celebration

Enlist the aid of the parish teachers. Ask them to have children of the parish school or religious education classes cut out fish from various colors of construction paper. On each fish, write a virtue—patience, fortitude, charity, etc. Let the children pass these out after the homily or put them in large baskets at the church doors and invite parishioners to take one as they leave Mass.

Meditation

Fishing can be frustrating! We human beings usually like to feel that we're in control of a situation; but when you go fishing, you can't make the fish bite. You can get the best kind of fishing rod and bait, your hook just right, and then try to find the perfect fishing hole, but there's no guarantee you'll catch anything.

Life can be that way too. No matter how hard you try to be in control, you just can't always land that big job or reel in the deal you want. So we often feel like saying, as Peter did, "Master, we've been hard at it all night and have caught nothing." Today our altar decorations remind us that we, too, can be fishers of men and that even when we grow tired, we must still have enough faith to be willing to cast out into deep waters and lower our nets again and again.

First Sunday of Lent

Deuteronomy 26: 4-10
Romans 10: 8-13
Luke 4: 1-13

Jesus was led by the Spirit into the desert for forty days where he was tempted by the devil.

Decoration

Use a low table covered with a purple or black cloth. Center it with a low basket filled with wood chips, that is, the brown bark used as a decorative ground cover in gardens or around patios (you should be able to find this at a hardware store, garden supply shop or greenhouse). Glue together some of the wood chips to make candle holders for two large purple candles or vigil lights, and place these on each side of the basket.

Addition—Make five Lenten banners for the five Sundays of Lent using purple and white felt or similar material that will be strong enough to hang properly. These will be most effective if you can hang them down the center aisle. If this is not possible, hang them behind the altar. You could hang all 5 banners today, or hang only one and add one on each Sunday of Lent. (See illustrations on pages 44-45.)

Celebration

When the priest processes out after Mass, have one of the altar boys or ushers carry out the basket of wood chips and stand with it at the back of church. If there are other doors where parishioners will exit, have additional altar boys and/or ushers standing at them holding baskets of chips. Each parishioner should be given a chip as they leave the church. Parishioners should be asked, perhaps during the homily or announcements, to carry these with them all during Lent.

Reflection

We all know it's easy to have good intentions but hard to follow through with them. Recently, in a high school class, each teen was given a 5-pound sack of sugar with instructions to handle this as though it were a baby, caring for it 24 hours a day. At first, this was fun, like a game. But after a few days of constantly having the responsibility to either carry it with them or arrange for someone else to care for it, they learned how difficult commitment can be.

On this first Sunday in Lent, most of us have good intentions to spend this time before Easter in penance and prayer. But perhaps before the end of Lent, we might need a reminder of that commitment. Because of this, our altar decoration today is simply a basket filled with wood chips. These will be our reminders.

At the end of Mass, a basket of chips will be at the church door. We ask each of you to take one wood chip and carry it with you every day of Lent, as a daily reminder that we share in the burden of Christ's cross, but also in his promise of new life. We will ask you to return your wood chip on Passion Sunday as a symbol of your Lenten sacrifices. All the chips will then be put together to form a Good Friday cross, a symbol of our union with Jesus in his death and resurrection.

108"

18"   23" bar

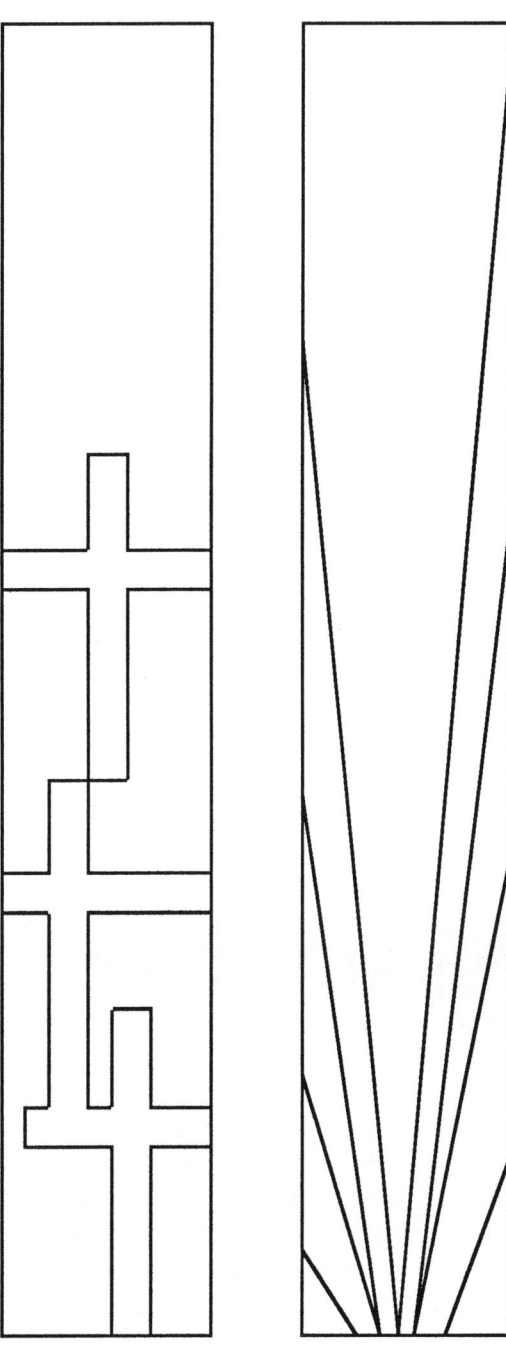

Each banner symbolizes a part of the passion. The first symbolizes the hill of Calvary where Jesus gave his human life to give us eternal life. The second banner depicts the crown of thorns and the third, the nails of the cross—reminders for us to offer up our suffering as Jesus did. The fourth banner shows the three crosses, reminding us that Jesus hung between two criminals who faced the kind of choice we all do in life. One cursed Jesus, the other asked for his help. The final banner illustrates light in the gloom. In the darkness of Lent, we have the promise of the light of Easter morning.

Second Sunday of Lent

Genesis 15: 5-12, 17-18
Philippians 3: 17—4, 1 or 3: 20-4
Luke 9: 28-36

He will give a new form to this lowly body of ours and remake it according to the pattern of his glorified body.

Decoration

Find long sheets of brown wrapping paper. Ask two children, wearing jeans or slacks, to lie down on the paper, with arms straight down and legs slightly apart. Trace around the figures, then cut out the design. You will have rather crude patterns of two people. (If the paper is wide enough, you could ask one child to bend an arm or leg to make the two designs a little different.) Use the purple or black background cloth that you used last week and center it with the basket again, this time, with just a few wood chips in it. Then put one of the wrapping-paper patterns on either side of the basket.

Addition—You will not need additional banners if you hung the five suggested last week. If you chose not to use those, you could make a mobile of "pattern" figures. Or a banner with a pattern design and the words, "Remake us, Lord Jesus, according to your pattern."

Celebration

In former years, most churches had a "poor box." Into these, people could drop a small donation that the St. Vincent de Paul Society or other parish group would use to help poor families. For this Sunday, find a sturdy box and cover it with felt or decorate it with a Lenten design. Have a slot where donations can be inserted and label it, "Lenten Poor Box. All donations will be used to help needy families." (You will probably need to arrange for someone to take the box from church after each Mass and remove the donations.)

Reflection

Today's second reading tells us that "we have our citizenship in heaven...there...the Lord Jesus Christ will give us a new form according to his pattern...." Lent provides each of us the opportunity to try to change our ways, to redesign the pattern of our life so that it will more closely resemble the pattern of life which Jesus has given us.

Third Sunday of Lent

Exodus 3: 1-8, 13-15
1 Corinthians 10: 1-6, 10-12
Luke 13: 1-9

An angel of the Lord appeared to him in fire flaming out of a bush. As he looked on, he was surprised to see that the bush, though on fire, was not consumed.

Decoration
Are you ready to build a burning bush? You could use flames made of red and orange felt. Or you could conceal a large, heavy-duty flashlight (with good batteries in it) inside a brown pot or earthenware container, then stuff the container with lots of red and orange cellophane cut with jagged edges. The light from the flashlight will shine up through the cellophane and resemble fire. Put this on a brown or beige burlap background and set a pair of men's sandals next to it. (Why? Because God told Moses to remove his sandals.)

Addition—Either the Lenten banners mentioned before or a banner with the design of flames and the words, "The bush, though on fire, was not consumed."

Celebration
With the theme of fire and Lent, this is the perfect time for evangelization. Perhaps some parish organization could make it their Lenten project to actively seek out parishioners who have not been coming to Mass and encourage them to come to church during Lent. Remind them of the times of Masses, or offer them a ride to Mass or another parish function.

Reflection
In today's first reading, Moses is surprised to see that the bush, though on fire, was not consumed. During Lent, we too should be on fire with new fervor and love of God. This is the fire that can comfort and warm without consuming.

This is also a fire that can and should be shared. If you have a neighbor or relative or friend who has not been coming to church, tell them about our Lenten schedule of Masses. Invite them to come with you. Encourage them to come back home for Lent.

Fourth Sunday of Lent

Joshua 5: 9, 10-12
2 Corinthians 5: 17-21
Luke 15: 1-3, 11-32

If anyone is in Christ, he is a new creation.

Decoration

Go to a hardware store and get two lengths of a very heavy-looking chain. Ask them to give you one broken link. On a plain purple background, arrange the two pieces of chain, with the broken link in the middle as though someone has broken free.

Addition—The Lenten banners, or two banners with the design of a broken chain, the first worded, "If anyone is in Christ, that person is a new creation," and the second lettered, "Your brother was dead and has come back to life."

Celebration

Consider having a Lenten Communion breakfast. Announce it ahead of time and take reservations. You could make it simpler by ordering take-out breakfasts from a restaurant. (Many of them will even deliver a large order at the time you specify if you give them a few days advance notice.) Add coffee and juice or milk for the children. Invite a speaker to make a short talk after breakfast on a topic that would be interesting and appropriate to the Lenten season.

Reflection

Today's altar decoration of a broken chain illustrates the Gospel story of the prodigal son. He left his father's house to go his own way and live his own life, but then broke away from that sinful life to return to his father, who welcomed him with open arms. The broken chain is also a reminder of the second reading in which Paul tells us, "If anyone is in Christ, he is a new creation." This theme of breaking free, newness and return to God is just what we work toward during Lent—breaking old habits, seeking new life, admitting when we are prodigal and returning home.

FIFTH SUNDAY OF LENT

Isaiah 43: 16-2
Philippians 3: 8-14
John 8: 1-11

Let the man among you who has no sin be the first to cast a stone...

Decoration

A simple purple background with a pile of rocks of various sizes.

Addition—The Lenten banners. Or a mobile made with various types of colored rocks. Or a banner with the design of rocks and the words, "who among you has no sin...cast the first stone..."

Celebration

Since this is the last Sunday of Lent and there will be many activities during Holy Week, it would be best to plan no celebration this week.

Reflection

As we draw near to the end of Lent, our simple altar decoration reminds us of the words of the Gospel, "Let he who is without sin cast the first stone." Lent has made us aware of our own sinfulness; but has it also made us aware of others' goodness? Are we more open to accept others without being judgmental? When we look at others do we try to see them as Jesus would have seen them?

In today's second reading, Paul says he is not done with his course nor reached the finish line. But he says, "I give no thought to what lies behind but push on to what is ahead." Although much of Lent is behind us, we can still push on to the finish line, making the most of the days remaining. You will remember that on the First Sunday of Lent, we each took home a wood chip to carry with us as a Lenten reminder. Please return your wood chip next Sunday so we can prepare our unity cross for Holy Week.

Passion Sunday
(PALM SUNDAY)

Isaiah 50: 4-7
Philippians 2: 6-11
Luke 22: 14-23, 56 or 23: 1-49

Taking bread and giving thanks, he broke it and gave it to them...he did the same with the cup...

Decoration

The palms can be your main decoration today. Make a fan-shaped arrangement by anchoring them in florists' clay, styrofoam, or a sturdy wire form positioned in a low bowl. Or arrange them in two tall vases the way you would arrange long-stemmed flowers. Use a white cloth, possibly edged in lace, as the background. In front of the fan, or between the two vases, put a small loaf of bread or a roll, broken in half, and a clear goblet of wine, only half-full.

Addition—Have vases of palms on the side altars. Or take small bunches of palms and tie them with white satin ribbon and attach them to every other pew down the center aisle, the way a florist attaches flowers to the pew ends for weddings. You could also add a white banner with the design of green palms and the words, "The king of Glory comes."

Celebration

Today offers a variety of possibilities for the solemn entrance procession. Your pastor may wish to invite the entire congregation to gather outside church and process in, carrying palms. Or you may choose to have a representative group from the parish do the same, perhaps the catechumens or parish council. If a solemn procession is not planned, perhaps you could ask some children to carry palms and process in with the celebrant, recalling the antiphon "...children waving palm branches ran out to welcome him..."

Reflection

Holy Week begins today in triumph as Jesus enters Jerusalem and is greeted with hosannas from the people and with children waving palms to praise and welcome him—in much the same way as we might today, with marching bands, confetti, and cheering crowds. Throughout this week, we will come to know Jesus' suffering and death before another triumphant Sunday dawns to the news that he has risen from the dead, and has turned defeat into victory.

As you take home a palm today, we ask you to please leave behind the wood chip which you have carried throughout Lent as a daily reminder of our share in the burden of Christ's cross. Baskets will be at the door of the church to collect them. Your wood chip will be united with those of everyone in our parish and school to form the cross for the celebration of the Lord's passion this Friday.

Holy Thursday

On this night, the only decorations you will need will be jugs of water, towels, and whatever else you may feel is necessary for the washing of the feet. This action best symbolizes our service to one another and the world.

Good Friday

To make an Easter Cross from the wood chips, first make the shape of a cross from plywood. Next, glue on the chips, using a heavy-duty glue such as Liquid Nails. (Be sure to completely cover the background.) If the people have forgotten to return all the chips, you may have to add additional ones in order to make the completed cross. If you hang it against a wall, you need cover only the front; but if you plan to carry it or display it standing, you will have to cover all sides.

You might wish to drape a long piece of purple cloth on the cross for Good Friday and change it to a white drape for Easter Sunday. If you have a thorn bush, rose bush, or pyracantha, use the branches to make a crown of thorns to add to the cross (make sure you wear gloves while making the crown!).

Holy Saturday

Some parishes have a celebration on Easter Saturday morning or afternoon to bless the Easter food. Families are invited to bring baskets of food which they will serve as part of the Easter feast—eggs, ham, bread, and the like. Some families will wish to decorate their baskets. Some will wish to have the children dress in Easter finery and carry the baskets. This short ceremony focuses on the blessing of the food by the priest (or another appropriate minister).

The Easter vigil celebration will depend on your particular parish. Decorations will be those for Easter Sunday. If you begin the liturgy in the evening, you might invite those attending to stay afterward for coffee and Easter cake. (Get sheet cakes and have them decorated with Easter designs.) If you begin the liturgy so that it will end near dawn, you can plan a simple Easter breakfast of coffee, juice, ham biscuits, scrambled eggs. Or you might choose to have only boiled eggs and coffee.

Easter Sunday

Acts 10: 34, 37-4
Colossians 3: 1-4 or 1 Corinthians 5: 6-8
John 20: 1-9

Early in the morning...while it was still dark, Mary Magdalene came to the tomb. She saw that the stone had been moved away...Simon Peter...observed the wrappings on the ground....

Decoration

Build a "stone wall" to suggest a cave. Use a piece of plywood approximately the length and height of the altar and paint on the shapes of large stones, using shadings of gray and white. Position this in front of and leaning against the altar for support. On each side, to cover the ends of the "wall," put lots of bushy green plants (like schefflera). At the center of the "stones," drape a long white cloth to look like a

winding sheet that has been left behind. It should wind down away from the stones, trailing across the carpet or down the altar steps. Place the crown of thorns (see Good Friday) on or near the cloth. Since the Easter lily is such a traditional part of this feast, you could put banks of these on the side altars.

Addition—Make a large horizontal banner or cut out large letters to form the word "Rejoice." Position this at the back of the church above the doorway so people will see it as they leave church after the Easter celebration.

Celebration

This is the one day when the liturgy itself is so much a celebration that you will not want to plan anything additional; most people will be going home to celebrate with their families. If your parish has many singles, widowed, divorced, elderly, and the like, who may have no celebration to attend, it would be a nice idea to arrange for an Easter brunch or Dutch Treat get-together at a nearby restaurant. You would need to announce it ahead of time, take reservations, make arrangements with the restaurant, and plan carpools.

Reflection

The tomb is empty! As our altar decorations show—Jesus Christ is risen today! Alleluia! Let us take this thought with us and keep it within our hearts so that we, too, may rise up and renew our lives.

Jesus died to save us. Let us rejoice that we are so loved. Jesus has risen from the dead to give us the promise of eternal life. Let us exult in this hope and this promise. And—as Mary Magdalene and the Apostles did—let us go forth to tell this good news to all who have ears to hear.

Second Sunday of Easter

Acts 5: 12-16
Revelation 1: 9-11, 12-13, 17-19
John 20: 19-31

Blest are they who have not seen and have believed.

Decoration
You may decide to leave the Easter decorations for today. If not, use a low table covered with a cloth of royal blue, deep green, or some bright color to show off a display of eyeglasses. Use whatever you can gather—children's glasses, adults' spectacles, sunglasses, or reading glasses. You might add a small telescope or microscope, and you'll probably want to use a bit of greenery to finish the arrangement.

Addition—If you have leftover easter lilies, put these at the sides of the arrangement. Or—if you keep the entire Easter decoration, you could just add a mobile made of various types of spectacles and hang it in the center aisle, or hang it near a side altar next to a banner lettered "Blest are they who have not seen and have believed."

Celebration
Today's meditation will invite parishioners to take home a pamphlet, so be sure that your parish pamphlet rack is well-stocked. If you don't have a pamphlet rack, consider buying one to keep permanently in the vestibule. Ask some parish couple to take charge of it as a ministry, keeping it in order, collecting the money from the money box, and ordering new titles. If this is not possible, contact a publisher or nearby religious goods store, and order a small assortment of books and/or pamphlets to display and sell today. They will usually let you buy on consignment so you can return whatever you don't sell.

Reflection

When you have trouble with your eyesight, you can shop around and find a lot of things to help you see better. As our altar decoration indicates, you can get reading glasses, bifocals with designer frames, fancy sunglasses, microscopes, telescopes, and many other items to improve your vision. But today's story of doubting Thomas shows us that we need more than that; we need the eyes of faith to see the truth, to hear the word of God and to believe.

The church also offers many things to help us "see" better—Scripture study groups, religious education programs, religious books. And if you say you're too busy for that, you can still find a lot of information in a pamphlet or book. Stop in the vestibule today, and take home one of these inexpensive, easy-to-read sources. You might find an answer to some "doubting Thomas" questions—you might find a way to "improve your vision."

Third Sunday of Easter

Acts 5: 27-32, 40-41
Revelation 5: 11-14
John 21: 1-19 or 21: 1-14

The Sanhedrin ordered the apostles not to speak again about the name of Jesus...the apostles left the Sanhedrin full of joy that they had been judged worthy of ill-treatment for the sake of the Name.

Decoration

Remember how children used to play telephone with two tin cans? Take two tin cans and cut out one end of each. Pierce a hole in each of the other can ends and tie a string to run from one can to the other. Use this as the centerpiece for your arrangement, then flank it with two or more telephones. If you don't have the kind of telephone you can unplug, ask a friend or a store to let you borrow some, possibly in different colors. As usual, finish up the arrangement with a bit of greenery.

Addition—How about a banner using the design of a telephone and the words, "Reach out and touch someone...."

Celebration

Does your parish have a "prayer chain?" If so, remind parishioners of it today. If not, begin one. Set up a card table in the vestibule, and ask someone to sit there with a sign-up sheet to explain how it works to anyone who is interested.

A prayer chain works like this: Get a number of people to volunteer to pray for the sick of the parish. Make up a list of the pray-ers' names and phone numbers. Each week in the bulletin, put in a notice similar to this: "If you would like someone to help you pray for a friend or relative who has a problem or illness, contact our parish prayer chain. Call Jane Doe at 123-4567." When the person who seeks prayers calls the chairperson, Jane Doe, she will call the second person on the list and the second will call the third, and so on down the list.

In this way the whole "chain" prays that day for whatever intention is requested.

Reflection

When you hear good news, you just can't wait to share it with someone. You usually hurry to the telephone and call your family and friends to tell them what just happened. That's the same way the apostles felt about Jesus' resurrection. They just couldn't wait to tell everybody. But in our first reading today, we hear that the high priest questioned them and told them to stop talking about Jesus. Yet this didn't bother the apostles. The reading tells us that they were "full of joy that they had been ill-treated for the sake of Jesus' name." Our altar decoration of telephones reflects this reading.

Homily or Bulletin Announcement

We'd like to invite you to join our parish prayer chain. Whenever anyone needs prayers for an illness or a problem, they call the first person on the chain, who then calls the second, who calls the third, until the whole "chain" is praying for that intention. If you would like to join this prayer chain or ask for prayers, there is a sign-up sheet today in the vestibule. Or you can call _____ at _____ for more information.

Fourth Sunday of Easter

Acts 13: 14, 43-52
Revelation 7: 9, 14-17
John 10: 27-30

My sheep hear my voice. I know them and they follow me.

Decoration

Try to find a rug or piece of fake fur or even a bath mat that resembles sheep wool and use this as your background. Center a statue or a picture of the Good Shepherd and flank it with candelabra holding red candles. Perhaps add some red flowers. If you can't locate a statue, you could use toy lambs or something similar (try to find ones that look realistic rather than cute).

Addition—Make a mobile with small sheep cut from white felt or wood, or made with cotton balls. Or use a banner with the words, "We are Jesus' people, the sheep of his flock," or one with the words, "I know my sheep, and mine know me."

Celebration

Have a get-acquainted coffee after Mass. Serve sweet rolls or donuts or cookies shaped like lambs. Or you could use those Easter lamb cake pans and make several lamb cakes to serve. On the serving table, have a toy lamb surrounded by flowers.

Following the idea of "I know mine and mine know me," try to get people to talk to people they have not met. To encourage this, you could have name tags so it will be easy to learn others' names. You could also appoint a few "greeters" who will chat with newcomers and introduce people to each other.

Reflection

Today's responsorial psalm reminds us, "we are his people, the sheep of his flock." The second reading mentions people of every nation and race whose robes had been washed white in the blood of the Lamb. And the Gospel tells us that Jesus said, "My sheep hear my voice. I know them and they follow me." So of course our altar decorations carry out the theme of the Good Shepherd. This is a comforting image. When you are depressed or lonely or discouraged, keep up your courage. You are not alone. Even if you stray and get lost, the Good Shepherd will search for you to bring you home.

Homily or Bulletin Announcement

Jesus said, "I know my sheep and mine know me." Do *you* know the other sheep in this flock, in your own parish? Look around the church and see how many you really know, how many you pray for, and share their troubles. Today, after Mass, we will have a get-acquainted Good Shepherd Coffee. Join us in the church hall and instead of visiting with the people you already know, introduce yourself to the ones you don't know.

Fifth Sunday of Easter

Acts 14: 21-27
Revelation 21: 1-5
John 13: 31-33, 34-35

I give you a new commandment: Love one another. Such as my love has been for you, so must your love be for each other."

Decoration
Although it isn't February 14, this is the day for a "hearty" decoration. Look through your leftover Valentine decorations; use whatever you can find that is heart-shaped or decorated with red hearts. If you don't have any leftovers, use a white table cloth with a runner of greenery. Cut out small red paper hearts and put them all along in the greenery like flowers. Turn two glass goblets upside down and use these as candle holders for two fat red candles. At the center of the greenery, prop up (with florist's clay or easels) two or more heart-shaped metal cake pans. If this does not seem full enough, add an arrangement of red and white flowers behind the cake pans.

Addition—A mobile of small red hearts. A white banner with the words, "A new commandment: love one another." A red banner with the words, "They'll know we are Christians by our love."

Celebration

Ask the school children or some parish organization to cut out enough red construction paper hearts for all parishioners. Type up as many Scripture sayings as you can find that include the word "love" or "heart." (You can find these in a concordance.) Type the Scripture quotes directly on the hearts, or you can type the quotes on a separate piece of paper, so that they will fit on the heart shapes. (Once you have a page full, you can copy it to make as many quotes as you will need.) Cut these out and paste one on each heart. Put these in baskets and have children stand at the church doors and give one to each person as they leave after Mass.

Reflection

In today's Gospel, Jesus says: "Such as my love has been for you so must your love be for each other." Today's heart-filled altar decoration reflects the idea of this simple direction which, if truly followed by all people at all times, could turn our world into one of complete happiness and joy. Jesus also said, "This is how they will know you as my disciples, by your love for one another." When people look at you and the way you live your life can they tell immediately that you are one of Jesus' disciples? Today let us all resolve to live so that others will truly know we are Christians by our love.

Sixth Sunday of Easter

Acts 15: 1-2, 22-29
Revelation 21: 10-14, 22-23
John 14: 23-29

Peace is my farewell to you, my peace is my gift to you...do not be distressed or fearful...I go away for a while and I come back to you....

Decoration

This week concentrate on a decoration behind the altar instead of in front of it. Make a huge banner, possibly using white felt, or a white bed sheet, or some other white cloth. Paint clouds on it in shades of gray and blue. In the center, letter the word "peace" with golden rays shooting from it. (Note: This decoration will also be appropriate for the feast of the Ascension this week.)

Addition—You will not need any additional banners, but if you want to add something in front of the altar you could use a simple fan-shaped arrangement of white flowers.

Celebration

You might plan to have a communal penance service this week. At one time, the church required that we satisfy our "Easter duty" by going to confession and communion at least once between Ash Wednesday and Trinity Sunday. Although this is no longer mandatory, the church does require all members to receive the eucharist at least once a year, and does recommend that you receive the sacrament of Reconciliation frequently to maintain a healthy spiritual life.

Reflection

There is often sadness mixed with joy when someone leaves on a trip. When a child leaves for college, there is joy over a new adventure, a new plateau of life; but there is also sadness for the family at the thought of being separated. Even when someone leaves for a long vacation, although it is a happy occasion, those waving goodbye may have tears in their eyes, already missing the one who will be away. In today's Gospel, Jesus explains that he must go away for a while but he tells his disciples to not be distressed or fearful. As our altar decoration shows, he promises them—and thus promises us, too—a farewell gift of Peace.

Seventh Sunday of Easter

Acts 7: 55-60
Revelation 22: 12-14. 16-17, 20
John 17: 20-26

I am the Alpha and the Omega, the First and the Last, the Beginning and the End.

Decoration

Find a book with a large picture of Jesus. Position it on a bookstand or easel as the center of the decoration. Place a strip of wide velvet ribbon in it like a bookmark. Cover the page opposite the picture with a heavy piece of paper on which you have lettered, "The First and the Last." To the left of the picture, put the Greek letter for Alpha; to the right, put the Greek letter for Omega (both can be cut from heavy cardboard.) Add greenery interspersed with vigil lights as a background.

Addition—Banner lettered "The Root and Offspring of David." A second banner lettered "The Morning Star shining bright."

Celebration

Try to get a big batch of stationery (the personal kind that you would use to write a letter to a friend), enough to have a sheet for every person at every Mass this Sunday. Pass it out at the door after Mass (see *Homily or Bulletin Announcement*).

Reflection

Our second reading and altar decorations remind us today that Jesus is the alpha and the omega, the first and the last, the beginning and the end. The Gospel tells us that Jesus wants us to be one with him, as he is one with God the creator. But how can you be one with someone you don't know? Since Jesus has invited us to be friends, we must nourish this friendship just as we would a human friendship.

Homily or Bulletin Announcement

When you want to be friends with someone, you get to know each other, then keep in touch. To help you "keep in touch" with Jesus, we invite you today to write a letter to him. After Mass, at the doors of the church, we will distribute sheets of stationery. Take one home and write a personal letter telling Jesus who you are, what you want from life, what bothers you or hurts you or worries you. Ask Jesus, the alpha and the omega, to truly be your best friend.

Pentecost Sunday

Acts 2: 1-11
1 Corinthians 12: 3-7, 12-13
John 20: 19-23

There are different gifts but the same spirit.

Decoration

Use a plain white cloth on the low table today. Center it with seven gift packages, each wrapped in a different wrapping paper. Use ferns or other greenery on each end of the table rather than flowers, so as not to detract from the colorful gifts.

Addition—Use one banner with the design of gift boxes and the words "Different gifts...the same spirit." Use another banner with the design of tongues of fire and the words, "Different ministries...the same Lord."

Celebration

Have representatives of several parish ministries on the altar or in the front pews where they can be introduced. Use this occasion to ask for volunteers to help with ministries such as lectors, choir members, ushers, catechists, and the like. You can either ask the representatives to say just a few words about their work or you can announce that they will be in the back of church after mass with sign-up sheets for volunteers.

Reflection

Today, on the happy feast of Pentecost, our altar decoration includes seven gift packages to symbolize the seven gifts of the Spirit—wisdom, understanding, counsel, fortitude, knowledge, piety and fear of the Lord. The packages also reflect the words of the second reading, "There are different gifts but the same Spirit; there are different ministries but the same Lord." On this day the apostles were filled with the Spirit. We too, as members of God's family, are filled with the Spirit. We don't all have the same gifts but we do each have gifts that we can share with other members of our church family.

In this parish, there are many ministries, many ways to serve the Lord. We would like to introduce a few of our parish members who participate in those ministries. (Introduce each by name, and perhaps ask each to speak briefly.) The second reading also says "to each person the manifestation of the Spirit is given for the common good." Be spirit-filled today and join in one of the parish ministries, so that you can share your gifts and your talents with your parish family.

Trinity Sunday

Proverbs 8: 22-31
Romans 5: 1-5
John 16: 12-15

...we boast of our hope for the glory of God...we even boast of our afflictions. We know that affliction makes for endurance, and endurance for tested virtue, and tested virtue for hope....

Decoration

To celebrate Trinity Sunday, make an arrangement with baskets of golden clover-leaf rolls plus pots of oxalis, the plant better known as the shamrock. (Oxalis has tiny white flowers and an obvious three-in-one leaf that is larger than the shamrock plants often found in the stores before St. Patrick's Day.) This shamrock has become a rather popular house plant, so you might be able to borrow some. If not, a greenhouse should be able to provide you with several pots if you contact them ahead of time. You could use one basket of rolls surrounded by plants, or one plant with a basket of rolls on each side. Add three white or green candles grouped on each side of the arrangement.

Addition—Make a large banner to go behind the altar lettered "Glory be to the Father, the Son and the Holy Spirit." Or you could keep the banner from Pentecost behind the altar and make a small banner for the side or make a poster with these words and incorporate it into the shamrock arrangement.

Celebration

Does your parish have any handicapped parishioners? If so, appoint a committee to consider their needs. Are there children in wheelchairs who cannot attend religious education programs, because the classrooms are inaccessible? Are there mentally retarded children who have not received First Communion because there are no teachers to prepare them? Do you need to add ramps or handicap parking spaces to make it easier to get into the church for Mass? Is there a parish couple who can never spend an evening out alone because they care for a handicapped child or relative, and is there someone who could stay with the handicapped person to give the parents a free evening or weekend?

Reflection

Today as we honor the Father, the Son and the Holy Spirit, our altar decorations celebrate the three-in-one mystery of the Trinity. In today's second reading, Paul tells us "we boast of our hope for the glory of God. But not only that—we boast of our afflictions." Do you "boast" of your afflictions or complain about them? Do you see affliction as an opportunity or as a stumbling block?

Homily or Bulletin Announcement

Although most of us have only minor afflictions, some of our handicapped parishioners have serious ones. Perhaps we have not given them as much consideration as we should. A new committee is being formed to study ways that we can better serve our physically or mentally handicapped parishioners. If you could offer suggestions or help, please call_____at_____.

THE BODY AND BLOOD OF CHRIST
(CORPUS CHRISTI)

Genesis 14: 18-20
1 Corinthians 11: 23-26
Luke 9: 11-17

We have nothing but five loaves and two fishes...they ate until they had enough...what they had left, over and above, filled twelve baskets.

Decoration

Make an arrangement of 12 baskets. Use 12 all alike, stacked two or three deep and interspersed with a bit of greenery. Or use 12 very different baskets of various sizes and styles. Or—if you don't think this would be too extreme—use the 12 baskets, six on each side of the arrangement, and in the middle put a loaf of bread with two cans of tuna fish!

Addition—Two banners—one red or purple with white lettering that spells out "This is my body," the other white with red or purple lettering, "This cup is the new covenant."

Celebration

Suggest that, in celebration of the miracle of the loaves and fishes, your parish collect canned goods to share with the "multitude" of today's poor. Announce that 12 baskets will be placed in the vestibule in the hopes that all can be filled by the following Sunday. Ask the St. Vincent de Paul Society or some other parish group to distribute the food to a local poor parish.

Reflection

Imagine that some good friends drop by unexpectedly. You are glad to see each other, and enjoy a nice visit with lots of good conversation. Then, it's lunch time. You'd like to share a meal but the only thing you have on hand is a loaf of bread and a few cans of tuna. Good friends aren't picky, so you make some sandwiches and enjoy more good conversation. When you've finished your lunch, there's even some tuna left over!

Today's Gospel tells of the time when Jesus had only five loaves and two fishes to feed the multitude. Yet they all ate until they had enough, and what was left over filled 12 baskets. Today's altar decoration includes 12 baskets, to remind us that if we trust in God's friendship and grace, we usually find that we have more than enough to see us through.

Homily or Bulletin Announcement

After Mass today, we will place 12 baskets in the vestibule. We invite you to bring canned goods this week or next Sunday so we can fill these baskets and distribute them to some of the "multitude" of poor in our city.

Sixth Sunday in Ordinary Time

Jeremiah 17: 5-8
1 Corinthians 15: 12, 16-20
Luke 6: 17, 20-26

Cursed is the man who trusts in human beings...whose heart turns away from the Lord. He is like a barren bush in the desert that enjoys no change of season....Blessed is the man who trusts in the Lord, whose hope is in the Lord. He is like a tree planted beside the waters that stretches out its roots to the stream.

Decoration
Find a dead branch or bush and "plant" it in a large pot. Place it on a slightly crumpled piece of sand-colored fabric to simulate the desert. Set it next to a large, fresh green plant or small tree, placed on a bright blue cloth to simulate the stream.

Addition—Poster made with water colors, using the design of a dead branch and the words, "Whose heart turns away from the Lord is like a barren bush...." Second poster showing a bright green tree and the words, "Whose hope is the Lord is like a tree planted beside the waters...."

Celebration
Purchase a large supply of greenery that can be cut into small sprigs and will stay fresh. If this is not possible, perhaps you could use artificial greenery. Place these in baskets and ask school children to stand at the church doors after Mass, holding the baskets, and pass out a green sprig to each parishioner to take home.

Reflection
Be not afraid. Today's altar decoration draws our atten-

tion to the first reading which tells us that those who seek strength in flesh and turn away from God will be like a barren bush. Those who trust God, who hope in God, are like a tree planted beside the waters. When the heat comes, its leaves stay green. When there is drought, it shows no distress. In today's world, we often face the heat of temptation and the drought of despair but trust and hope that God will refresh us and keep our faith evergreen, so that it may flourish and yield good fruit.

Seventh Sunday in Ordinary Time

1 Samuel 26: 2, 7-9, 12-13, 22-23
1 Corinthians 15: 45-49
Luke 6: 27-38

...the measure you measure with will be measured back to you.

Decoration
Put together a grouping of measuring devices—a tape measure, a yardstick, a ruler, various sizes and shapes of kitchen measuring cups. For a background, you could use a kitchen tablecloth or a strip of bright-colored felt, any fabric that will show off your arrangement.

Addition—Make a banner with an inch measure stitched down the side and the words, "The measure you measure with..." and a second banner with another measure stitched down the side, with the words, "...will be measured back to you." Instead of banners, you could hang one of those colorful "growth charts" that parents often hang in a child's room.

Celebration

Put a large box in the vestibule with a sign saying, "'Do not judge and you will not be judged...do not condemn and you will not be condemned.' Please leave offerings of reading material here, whether religious or otherwise, for distribution to prisons." Check ahead with a local jail or prison to see what type of reading material they will allow you to bring and then ask parishioners to donate these—possibly back issues of Catholic magazines, or various kinds of newspapers, pamphlets, and books. Appoint a small committee to gather and deliver these.

Reflection

Do you sometimes judge others too harshly or do you judge them fairly as you would wish others to judge you? Do you "take someone else's measure" too quickly or do you give them a chance to prove themselves? Today's altar decoration reflects the Gospel message, "For the measure you measure with will be measured back to you." This week, examine the way you judge family, friends, and acquaintances. Do your actions "measure up" to today's Gospel message "Be compassionate as your God is compassionate"?

EIGHTH SUNDAY IN ORDINARY TIME

Sirach 27: 4-7
1 Corinthians 15: 54-58
Luke 6: 39-45

When a sieve is shaken, the husks appear; so do a man's faults when he speaks.

Decoration

Make an arrangement centered with an opened dictionary. Surround it with such items as a sieve, a tea strainer, a colander, or a flour sifter. Use a colorful background or some greenery or flowers to complete the effect.

Addition—Make two banners with the design of a sieve or sifter with the words "sifting" out of the design. On the first banner, use the words, "When a sieve is shaken, the husks appear..." and on the second, "...so do one's faults when one speaks."

Celebration
This would be a good Sunday to have a small selection of Catholic books and pamphlets for sale in the vestibule after all Masses. Perhaps one of the parish groups can take charge of ordering the books, displaying them, and handling the sales. Parishioners might also want to buy and donate these books to the prisoner's box mentioned last Sunday. If all the books are not sold, perhaps the parish could donate some or all of the leftovers to the prison box. (This Sunday will sometimes occur in February. When it does, you can publicize your book sale by mentioning that February is Catholic Press Month.)

Reflection
How often do we speak first and think later! By doing this, we sometimes hurt others or misinform them. This is especially important when we are speaking about religion. Our altar decoration reflects the words of today's first reading "When a sieve is shaken, the husks appear...so do one's faults when one speaks." Most people continue learning and growing in other areas of their lives; but they often stop studying about God, the most important subject of all. In today's Gospel, Jesus says, "Can a blind man act as guide to a blind man?" We should all continue reading and trying to learn more about God so that when we speak, we will speak the truth and when we try to lead others, we will lead them in the right direction.

NINTH SUNDAY IN ORDINARY TIME

1 Kings 8: 41-43
Galatians 1: 1-2, 6-10
Luke 7: 1-10

...that all the peoples of the earth may know your name...and may acknowledge that this temple which I have built is dedicated to your honor.

Decoration
Buy a selection of small flags of various nations, and arrange them in a bowl as you would a flower arrangement, using greenery as a filler. If you can only find a few flags, then either make a flower arrangement or use a large fern and put a few flags in as highlights.

Addition—If you can find some large flags of other nations, hang them instead of banners or suspend them from the ceiling, spaced several feet apart, coming down the center aisle. And of course include the American flag. Or, make banners to look like flags and use the words, "That all the peoples of the earth may know your name...."

Celebration

Ask some parish children to dress in various ethnic outfits and bring up the gifts at the offertory. If there are ethnic families in the parish, they may have these outfits. If not, you may need to do a bit of research and a bit of improvising (i.e., a Dutch hat out of white posterboard, a Mexican-patterned scarf for a serape, green shamrocks on a white dress for Ireland).

Reflection

Our altar decorations today show flags of many nations (and, in the offertory procession, children are dressed in the costumes of foreign lands) because in our first reading today, Solomon prays "...that all the peoples of the earth may know your name." In the second reading, Paul is sending greetings afar, to the people known as Galatians. And in the Gospel, a centurion, who apparently is not one of Jesus' followers, is nevertheless asking Jesus to heal his servant.

We are reminded in many ways that the family of God includes people of other lands and other customs. We must open our hearts, our minds, our arms to welcome all, as God does. We must "go out to all the word and tell the good news."

Tenth Sunday in Ordinary Time

1 Kings 17: 17-24
Galatians 1: 11-19
Luke 7: 11-17

Jesus said..."I bid you get up." The dead man sat up and began to speak.

Decoration

Use two vases, one filled with dead, dry twigs and the other filled with flowering branches. Make them the same height and width to balance. In between the two vases, place some kind of shallow bowl, copper or crystal or ceramic. Put some small slips of paper and a few pencils near the bowl. Completely cover the table with white vigil lights but only light a few of them.

Addition—Banner with the words of today's responsorial psalm, "I will praise you, Lord, for you have rescued me."

Celebration

Although it has been a long-time Catholic custom to pray for the faithful departed, this custom has not been emphasized much in recent years. Today would be a good time to have a Holy Hour or an afternoon of prayer for our loved ones who have died. At the last Mass, invite all to stay after, or plan to leave the church open so that people can come in the afternoon. Invite them to write the name of a deceased loved one on a slip of paper and put it in the container by the altar. Then light a vigil light and stay to say a prayer.

Reflection

In today's Gospel, the people were amazed when Jesus took pity on the widowed mother and brought her son back from death to life. How much more amazing it is that Jesus has promised us all that death for us will lead to eternal life. Our altar decorations today show the dead branches and those that are radiant with life. Each Winter, the branches seem dead. Yet each Spring, they return to beautiful life, just as we will when we are reunited with God.

Homily or Bulletin Announcement

Most of us have a relative, an ancestor, or friend who has left the world as we know it. Today, we invite you to come up to the altar after Mass (or this afternoon) and take a slip of paper. Write down the name of your loved one who has died, then put the paper in the bowl, light a vigil light, and stay to say a prayer for all the faithful departed.

Eleventh Sunday in Ordinary Time

2 Samuel 12: 7-10
Galatians 2: 16, 19-21
Luke 7: 36—8: 3 or 7: 36-50

Two men owed money to a certain moneylender...one 500 coins...the other 50. Since neither was able to repay, he wrote off both debts. Which of them was more grateful to him?

Decoration
Try to find some balance scales, preferably the kind that have two sides of weights that balance against each other (e.g., the scales of justice). Make a velvet pouch tied at the top with a gold ribbon. Fill it with rocks or something similar that will look like a bag of 500 coins, and put it on one side of the scale. Make a smaller pouch, also tied at the top but filled with less weight—like the 50 coins—and put it on the other side of the scale. Use greenery and candles to complete the arrangement.

Addition—Banner with a coin design and the words "One owed 500...the other owed 50." A second banner with the words, "Your sins are forgiven."

Celebration
Suggest that people stay after Mass to say an Act of Contrition for their personal forgiveness, and a rosary for the intentions of those they have not forgiven.

Reflection
Today's altar decoration represents the Gospel story of two men who owed a moneylender. One owed 500 coins, the other only 50; but the moneylender forgave both. We all owe debts, some larger than others. But Jesus offers all of us forgiveness. Are you as generous?

Homily or Bulletin Announcement
Think today of the people in your life who you have not been able to forgive for past wrongs. Stay after Mass and make an Act of Contrition for your own sins. Then say a rosary or a decade of the rosary for the intention of those who have not been forgiven and for those who may most need forgiveness today.

Twelfth Sunday in Ordinary Time

Zechariah 12: 10-11
Galatians 3: 26-29
Luke 9: 18-24

Who do the crowds say that I am?

Decoration

Since we all wear many different hats, use a variety of them for today's decoration—a man's straw hat, golf cap, or a visor; a woman's fancy dress hat, gardening hat, or bridesmaid's hat; a child's cowboy hat, fireman's hat or Mickey Mouse hat. And if you know a priest or monsignor who has a biretta, borrow that.

Addition—One banner lettered "Who do the crowds say that I am?" Another lettered "Who do *you* say that I am?"

Celebration

How about having a "family photo" day today to echo the idea of "Who am I?" Ask several people to bring cameras (preferably Polaroids), and plenty of film. Set aside an area in the parking lot, or in the vestibule or church hall. Let families pose together, and take quick, candid shots. (You might collect a small fee—fifty cents or a dollar—to pay for the film.) Take some of the hats from the altar decoration and let people wear them for the photos.

Reflection

In today's Gospel, Jesus asked his friends, "Who do the crowds say I am?" and there were several answers to his question. Our altar decoration shows that we, too, may be seen in many ways, because in our busy world we all wear many hats. The "crowd" may see a man as a wage earner, a husband, father, Scout leader, bridge player. They may see a woman as a wage earner, wife, mother, carpool driver, golfer, or volunteer worker. Even children fill many roles—as a brother or sister, student, soccer player, or ballerina.

Jesus asked his friends, "Who do *you* say that I am?" Jesus knows the truth about each of us. He knows who we are, in all our dimensions, no matter what hat we are wearing. But do we know Jesus? Do we talk to him everyday as we would with a friend? Do we try to get to know Jesus better? When he asks, "Who do you say I am?" what do you answer?

Thirteenth Sunday in Ordinary Time

1 Kings 19: 16, 19-21
Galatians 5: 1, 13-18
Luke 9: 51-62

It was for liberty that Christ freed us....but not a freedom that gives free rein to the flesh.

Decoration
This Sunday will fall somewhere near our own day to celebrate liberty on July 4th, so make this a patriotic decoration. Use a red, white, or blue cloth, possibly even a paper one with a Fourth of July motif. Make an arrangement using red and white carnations or geraniums, or just white Queen Anne's lace. Mix in some small American flags, a bit of fern and maybe one or two large red firecrackers. This would show up nicely if you put them in a black kettle or coal scuttle, or maybe even a picnic basket.

Addition—Two banners using a red, white, and blue background, one with the words, "Christ called us to live in freedom"; the second with the words, "...but freedom calls for responsibility."

Celebration
Make a list of the names and addresses of all those who represent your area in federal or state government positions. Make enough copies for all parishioners, then put the lists in the pew racks or have someone hand them out after Mass.

Reflection
Our altar decorations today remind us of freedom and liberty because the second reading tells us "It was for liberty that Christ freed us." But the reading then goes on to explain that this does not mean a freedom that gives free rein to the flesh. We are told to serve one another, to live in accord with the spirit.

Homily or Bulletin Announcement

All too often we Americans take our liberty for granted without accepting the responsibility for it. One way we can serve one another is to use our influence to see that proper laws are enacted and enforced. We can do this by writing letters. In the back of the church today is a list of the names and addresses of the elected officials in our area. Please take home one of the lists. Use it to write and express your opinion, both to disapprove of official actions, and to applaud the good work being done.

Fourteenth Sunday in Ordinary Time

Isaiah 66: 10-14
Galatians 6: 14-18
Luke 10: 1-12, 17-20

On entering any house, first say, "Peace to this house."

Decoration
There are many beautiful wooden carvings or plaques that feature the word "shalom." Use one of these as the focal point of today's decoration. Complete the arrangement with some rustic touches—a burlap cloth, some rocks or pieces of firewood, and an arrangement of orange day lilies mixed with greenery. Instead of candles, use two green kerosene lamps.

Addition—Two burlap banners, one with the word "shalom," the other with the words "peace be with you."

Celebration

Suggest that today parishioners use each other's names at the Sign of Peace. If they don't know the names of the people around them they can introduce themselves, saying, for example, "My name is Mary. Peace be with you."

Reflection

In today's Gospel, those going out to spread the Good News are told that when they enter any house, they should first say, "Peace to this house." That's why our altar decoration focuses on the word "shalom," a Hebrew greeting that means "peace be with you." Today we ask you also to focus on what it truly means to offer peace to your neighbor.

The Gospel tells us that if a peaceable man receives your greeting, your peace will rest on him. If not, it will come back to you. Wherever you go this week, remember the words of the Gospel and bring peace to whatever house you enter—especially your own.

Fifteenth Sunday in Ordinary Time

Deuteronomy 30: 10-14
Colossians 1: 15-20
Luke 10: 25-37

A Samaritan...approached him and dressed his wounds....

Decoration

It's time for first aid and bandaids! Make a bank of greenery (ferns or ivy). Use a first-aid kit with a big red cross on it as the focal point. (Maybe you could find a toy doctor kit or nurse kit, or a Boy Scout first-aid kit.) Drape partially-unrolled gauze along the greenery, then add boxes of bandaids, pill boxes, and medicine bottles to the arrangement. (For safety's sake, don't have real medicine in the bottles.)

Addition—One banner at the front lettered, "Which of the three acted Christ-like?" and a banner at the back lettered "Go and do the same."

Celebration

Call local hospitals or nearby nursing homes and ask if they need volunteers, what type of service these volunteers would be expected to do, and what hours they are most needed. Make an announcement asking for volunteers. Copy a list of the names and phone numbers of places needing help, and distribute it during or after Mass. If your parish has a group that visits a hospital or nursing home regularly, announce the chairperson's name and phone number, asking parishioners to call for further information.

Reflection

We are all familiar with the Gospel story of the Good Samaritan, the man who helped someone in need when others simply passed by. Our altar decoration of first-aid supplies reminds us that there are many places today where people need our help.

Yet a one-time, hurry-up, bandaid-type of help is not always enough. There are many elderly lonely people who need a friend on a continuing basis. And there are many hospitals and nursing homes that have difficulty finding enough volunteer help. Could you give some time to be a Good Samaritan? Think about other ways that you could help your neighbors in need.

Sixteenth Sunday in Ordinary Time

Genesis 18: 1-10
Colossians 1: 24-28
Luke 10: 38-42

Mary seated herself at the Lord's feet and listened to his words....Martha was busy with all the details of hospitality.

Decoration
How about a rocking chair on the altar today? Set it next to a low table where you have arranged a pair of reading glasses, a teapot next to a cup and saucer, perhaps a plate of cookies, a plant, and several Catholic books and newspapers, including a small Bible. You might even hang a sweater or an apron on the back of the rocker.
Addition—Two banners, one lettered "Martha was busy...", the other lettered, "Mary was listening..."

Celebration
Ask one of the parish organizations to have a Catholic book sale today as a fundraiser. Most publishers will give you volume discounts, so that you can make a profit on each book you sell. Or invite one of the Catholic magazines (for example, *Today's Parish*) to send a representative to speak about their publication.

Reflection
Some people worry about today's Gospel story of Martha and Mary, wondering why Mary doesn't get up and help her busy sister. True hospitality is a form of Christian charity. But most of us would have to admit that we usually are too busy today to sit at the Lord's feet and listen to his words. Our altar decoration is an indication of how much good Catholic reading material is available. Take a little time each day away from television or other activities to read the Bible or a Catholic

book, magazine, or newspaper. Maybe then we will not be as anxious and upset as Martha was. Find time to sit at the Lord's feet and listen.

Seventeenth Sunday in Ordinary Time

Genesis 18: 20-32
Colossians 2: 12-14
Luke 11: 1-13

Give us this day our daily bread....

Decoration
Use a red-checkered cloth with a simple flower arrangement, possibly honeysuckle or daisies in a kitchen pitcher. Or use an electric mixer and put the flowers in the bowl part. Add several loaves of bread, plus a clear glass container of flour with a scoop in it, a large kitchen salt shaker, a bread board, and a bread knife. Use two round fat red candles, one set on top of a round can of shortening and the other on top of a round can of baking powder.
Addition —Use two banners, one lettered "...for the sake of ten" and the other lettered, "Give us this day our daily bread."

Celebration
Invite all to share a prayer breakfast. Serve only bread—e.g., raisin bread or cinnamon bread—plus coffee and juice. If the group is small, ask all to join hands and each say a short, spontaneous prayer. If it is a larger group, ask all to join hands and say the Our Father. You could also ask a few people ahead of time to prepare personal petitions or prayers.

Reflection
Each of today's readings speaks of prayer. In the first reading, Abraham bargains with God, praying for God to save the city if only ten innocent people can be found. In the second reading, Paul speaks of God pardoning our sins and in the Gospel, Jesus tells us how to pray to the Father. Our altar decoration suggests that we remember to pray every day—"Give us this day our daily bread." We, like Abraham, might find it

hard to name enough innocent people for our city to be spared. But we have hope because Jesus has told us, "Ask and you shall receive, seek and you shall find, knock and it shall be opened to you."

Homily or Bulletin Announcement
In keeping with the Gospel for today, you are all invited to the parish hall after Mass for a short prayer breakfast. There we will share bread and prayer.

Eighteenth Sunday in Ordinary Time

Ecclesiastes 1: 2; 2: 21-23
Colossians 3: 1-5, 9-11
Luke 12: 13-21

A man may be wealthy but his possessions do not guarantee him life.

Decoration

Make a bank of greenery, using ferns, ivy, or the like. Go through catalogs and home decorating magazines and cut out pictures of anything that illustrates extreme luxury—custom cars, mansions, lavish furnishings, furs, and jewels. Mount these on pieces of colored posterboard, pasting a piece of cardboard on the back, like an easel, to make it easier to stand them up. Position these among the greenery on one side. On the other, amidst the greenery, put photographs of families, an older couple (like grandparents), a children's baseball team or Scout group, a college graduate in a cap and gown—anything that illustrates relationships.

Addition—Two banners with these messages: "Possessions do not guarantee life" and "Grow rich in the sight of God."

Celebration

Take a piece of paper, and draw a vertical line down the center. On the top left, letter "material possessions"; on the top right, letter "real treasures." Make enough copies to leave in the pews, so that parishioners can take them home and list their "possessions." Or use a large piece of posterboard for the "list" and put it in front of the lectern and ask the assembly to write their own list when they get home.

Reflection

Today's readings—as well as our altar decoration—draw our attention to the true meaning of life. The first reading speaks of the "vanity of vanities," while the second reading says to "set your heart on what pertains to higher realms." The Gospel tells of the man who "grows rich for himself instead of growing rich in the sight of God."

What are the real "treasures" of life? Many people have valuable possessions like the ones on the left side of today's altar decoration. These are good, as long as you do not let such possessions possess you. But the true treasures are the ones pictured on the other side—family, children, education, community.

Homily or Bulletin Announcement

When you go home today, take a piece of paper and list your material possessions on one side. Then list your real "treasures" on the other. Which list is more important to you? Have you been growing rich in the eyes of the world instead of growing rich in the sight of God?

NINETEENTH SUNDAY IN ORDINARY TIME

Wisdom 18: 6-9
Hebrews 11: 1-2, 8-19 or 11: 1-2, 8-12
Luke 12: 32-48 or 12: 35-40

By faith Abraham obeyed when he was called...he went forth...not knowing where he was going...for he was looking forward to the city with foundations, whose designer and maker is God.

Decoration

Time to plan a trip! For your decoration today, use a road map on which you have clearly marked a route in heavy black magic marker. Add car keys, some folded road maps or a road atlas, an auto compass, flares, the kind of flashlight used to signal trouble—anything to indicate a journey, preparation, and plans. Add a small sign or banner lettered "Where are you going?"

Addition—Large banner behind the altar, lettered "Faith is confident assurance concerning what we hope for, and conviction about things we do not see."

Celebration

In the back of church, where it can be seen as people are entering or leaving, hang a large piece of posterboard lettered Parish Road Map. Draw a "route" on it and letter-in the various activities in your parish—Scripture study, parish school, religious education, daily Mass, Marriage Encounter, First Saturday rosary, and the like. Suggest that people spend this week making their own "Family Road Map."

Reflection

In today's first reading, Abraham obeyed "by faith," going forth, not knowing where he was going. Today, our altar decoration asks, "Where are you going?" When we take a trip, we usually plan ahead, charting our route on a map, taking along a compass, and following directions to our destination. But we can't always chart our life that way. We have to go forth in faith, trusting in God and having conviction about the things we do not see. We never know which turn the road will take or what's around the next curve. We do know that our final destination is with God; this faith makes our journey meaningful.

Homily or Bulletin Announcement
In the back of church, we have put a Parish Road Map. On it are some of the signs that help us head in the right direction, such as Scripture study, prayer, and ministries. This week, you might like to make a Family Road Map, putting down the things that have determined which direction your family will take—where you live, what kind of work you do, how many children you have, how you are involved in your parish, and what you do for fun. Look at your map carefully and check to see if you're going in the right direction.

Twentieth Sunday in Ordinary Time

Jeremiah 38: 4-6. 8-10
Hebrews 12: 1-4
Luke 12: 49-53

Persevere in running the race which lies ahead; let us keep our eyes on Jesus...remember how he endured the opposition of sinners; hence do not grow despondent or abandon the struggle.

Decoration
Get out the running shoes! Make an arrangement of tennis shoes, golf shoes, ladies' high heels, sandals, little girls' Mary Janes, and some toddler shoes. If you don't have room to use pairs, just use one of each to indicate variety. You might add greenery to hide some of the scuff marks!

Addition—Large banner with the words, "For the sake of the joy which lay before him, he endured the cross, heedless of its shame."

Celebration
How about a fun activity to emphasize today's idea of running the race? Make plans ahead to have an afternoon event that features various team races—children against teachers or the parish staff (including the priests), parents against teens, boys against girls, maybe even a sack race or a three-legged race. Have refreshments and silly prizes.

Reflection
Today's second reading tells us to "persevere in running the race." Our altar decoration reminds us of the old saying "You cannot judge a man until you have run a mile in his moccasins." We each run the race in different ways—some in high heels, some in tennis shoes, some even barefoot. But we must all persevere and keep our eyes fixed on Jesus. In

spite of opposition and ridicule and persecution, Jesus endured. We all encounter obstacles and stumbling blocks as we run the race of life; but we must not be despondent or discouraged. By following Jesus' example, we, too, can endure and triumph.

Twenty-First Sunday in Ordinary Time

Isaiah 66: 18-21
Hebrews 12: 5-7, 11-13
Luke 13: 22-30

When once the master of the house has risen to lock the door and you stand outside knocking and saying, "Sir, open for us," he will say in reply, "I do not know where you come from."

Decoration
Make the focus of today's decoration an assortment of keys. This would be a good time to use a mobile with different sizes and shapes of keys. If this is not possible, use key chains or many keys on one of those large key "bracelets" that can fit over your wrist, something that will be big enough to show up. Then make an arrangement of a Bible, a rosary, some prayer books, collection envelopes, a small statue of Jesus or the Holy Family, a crucifix, and vigil lights. Add a small sign lettered "Keys to the Kingdom."

Addition—Two banners, one lettered "There will be wailing and grinding of teeth..."; the other lettered "Some who are last will be first and some who are first will be last."

Celebration
Put a suggestion box in the back of church. Ask parishioners to really consider what the parish could do and is not doing, or could be doing better, to help parishioners find and use the keys to the kingdom. Ask for honest suggestions—not just problems but possible solutions.

Reflection
Today's second reading speaks of a subject that is not very popular in today's world: discipline. We are told "do not disdain the discipline of the Lord...nor lose heart when he re-

proves you...endure your trials...for what son is there whom his father does not discipline?" All parents know that if they truly love their children, they must discipline them, teach them, and guide them. The Gospel goes on to show us what can happen to us if we do not take advantage of this discipline. Jesus tells of the time when the master will lock the door of the house and many will stand outside knocking, wanting to come in, wailing.

Today's altar decoration shows that we are offered what might be called "keys" to the kingdom—Scripture, prayer, giving financial support to help the church, following the example of Jesus. These are the forms of discipline that can help us get inside the kingdom before the door is locked, before we are left outside, knocking, wailing, realizing that we have lost the keys, realizing we have waited too long.

Twenty-Second Sunday in Ordinary Time

Sirach 3: 17-18, 20: 28-29
Hebrews 12: 18-19, 22-24
Luke 14: 1, 7-14

Conduct your affairs with humility...humble yourself the more, the greater you are, and you will find favor with God.

Decoration
Try using several photographs of Mother Teresa, shown with the people she has helped and with the Sisters who follow in her footsteps. There are many books about her that have her picture on the cover; you could use these in your display. You could also borrow or copy photographs from the files of the local newspaper, or the area Catholic paper. Add yellow flowers and greenery to the display.

Addition—Instead of the arrangement above—or in addition to it—you could enlarge some of the pictures and hang them like banners, suspend them from the ceiling, or make a mobile of them hanging at different heights. Appropriate banners could be lettered "They who exalt themselves shall be humbled..." and "They who humble themselves shall be exalted."

Celebration
Ask the pastor of a poorer parish to speak today about some of the neediest families in his area. Invite your parish families to adopt a poorer family, and offer them friendship as well as material help. Or arrange for the parish as a whole to adopt one or more families, and help them on a continuing basis. You'll probably find that the families who give will benefit more from this program than the families who receive.

Reflection

Today's first reading and Gospel both advise us to lead our lives with humility. One person who has shown the modern world the virtue of humility has been Mother Teresa. She humbled herself to work with the dying, the poorest of the poor, the people who the world might see as undesirable. Mother Teresa and the sisters who continue her work have seen these people as beautiful in the eyes of the Lord. Let us pray today that we too will learn the humble art of helping and serving others, not because we are superior to them but because we are all brothers and sisters in the family of God.

Twenty-Third Sunday in Ordinary Time

Wisdom 9: 13-18
Philemon 9-10, 12-17
Luke 14: 25-33

Who knows God's counsel or who can conceive what the Lord intends?

Decoration
Here's a chance to use a replica of Rodin's sculpture, "The Thinker"—the man sitting with his head down, hand under chin, obviously deep in thought. Perhaps you can borrow one of these or get a photograph of one. Add a calculator, a telephone, a pad with some mathematical formulas written on it, and a pencil. If you can get a cardboard replica of a computer, that, too, would be appropriate. Use a background drape of satin or similar material and add greenery or flowers.

Addition—Two banners with these messages: "Who can know what the Lord intends?" and "Lord, teach us your ways."

Celebration
Rather than a parish celebration, use this week to ask each person to rethink his or her approach to decision-making and to determine to put more trust in the Lord.

Reflection
In today's push-button world, we have become accustomed to hurry-up decision-making. As our altar decoration indicates, we can usually get a fast solution by using a calculator or a computer, or by calling dial-an-answer. We no longer have the luxury to spend weeks or months thinking through a problem like the serious "thinker" might have in past generations.

Today's first reading reminds us that true wisdom is a gift

of God. When you have an important decision to make, do you base it solely on the world's guidelines and psychology? Or do you go to God and beg for guidance and wisdom?

This week, take some time out from the daily grind to do some quiet thinking. Think about whether you've been setting priorities and making decisions based solely on the kind of calculations that come from a computerized society. Is it time for you to put more trust in the Lord and "seek his counsel"?

Twenty-Fourth Sunday in Ordinary Time

Exodus 32: 7-11, 13-14
1 Timothy 1: 12-17
Luke 15: 1-32 or 15: 1-10

What woman, if she has ten silver pieces and loses one, does not light a lamp and sweep the house in a diligent search until she has retrieved what she lost? And when she finds it, she calls in her friends and neighbors to say, "Rejoice with me!"...There will be the same kind of joy...over one repentant sinner.

Decoration
Use a nice soft drape as a background with—yes!—nine silver pieces arranged in the center. You can use silver dollars, or half-dollars, or wrap buttons with foil to look like silver pieces. To one side, put a silver bowl filled with green broccoli and white flowers. (The broccoli has no significance; it would just look interesting instead of the usual greenery.) If you can get some sprays of a "silver dollar" plant to add to the arrangement, that would be ideal. (If you don't know anyone who grows these in the garden, you can usually get them at any store that sells dried flowers. When the leaf dries, it falls off and leaves an interior leaf that is paper-thin and looks like a round silver dollar.) On the other side of the flowers, put the one "lost" silver piece next to a lamp, possibly an old-fashioned coal-oil lamp. Stand a broom on each side, or lay one in the background or below the arrangement.

Addition—Banner proclaiming, "Rejoice! The lost has been found...the sinner saved!"

Celebration
Have you heard about the Reach Out to Inactive Catholics

program? If your parish hasn't tried it, this might be a good time to introduce it. The program gives a detailed plan to help the parish locate inactive Catholics in your area and invite them to the church for discussion. Also included is a "refresher" on the faith, designed to encourage a return to an active practice of their religion. You can find the book that details this program at a Catholic bookstore, or you can write to Ligouri Publications, Ligouri, MO 63057.

Reflection

Today's familiar Gospel story tells of the lost sheep and, as our altar decoration shows, of the woman who had 10 silver pieces but lost one. What did she do? She lit a lamp and swept the house, searching until the lost coin had been found. She then called in her friends to rejoice. Jesus tells us that in the same way, there is great rejoicing in heaven over one repentant sinner who has been "lost" and then is found.

Homily or Bulletin Announcement

Do you have a relative or friend or neighbor who is lost, searching, waiting for someone to come along and show them the way back? Sometimes we Catholics hesitate to discuss religion, to ask lapsed Catholics why they no longer attend Mass. Maybe we should. If you know any inactive Catholics, invite them to come to Mass with you next week. You may be surprised at their positive reaction. They may have just been waiting for someone to ask them to come home.

Twenty-Fifth Sunday in Ordinary Time

Amos 8: 4-7
1 Timothy 2: 1-8
Luke 16: 1-13 or 16: 10-13

No one can serve two masters...you cannot give yourself to God and money.

Decoration

Use sprays of real or artificial flowers. In among the flowers, to the right, place a Bible, propped so that it can be easily seen. To the left, place account books or large business ledgers, also propped up. Add large candles or two coal-oil lamps (as though you have been "burning the midnight oil").

Addition—Two banners, one lettered "No one can serve

two masters," the other lettered "My business partner is God."

Celebration
Write petitions to be said at the prayer of the faithful for business people, and those in positions of authority. You can personalize your prayers to include people from your area but you might use these for starters: For the President of the United States...For members of Congress...For lawyers...For accountants...For priests and bishops...and so on.

Reflection
Today's Gospel reminds us, "No one can serve two masters." Our altar decoration illustrates the laws of God on one side—the Bible—and the laws that rule business on the other side—account books and ledgers. Today's business world has become very complex and competitive. It is not always easy to be a successful business person and also a successful Christian. In today's second reading, Paul urges that "petitions, prayers, intercessions and thanksgivings be offered for all people, especially kings and those in authority." We don't have a king in our country but we do have many authority figures. Let us join today in prayer that they will lead wisely and well.

Twenty-Sixth Sunday in Ordinary Time

Amos 6: 1. 4-7
1 Timothy 6: 11-16
Luke 16: 19-31

Woe to the complacent...stretched comfortably on their couches...

Decoration

Here's an opportunity to use some of the handmade pillows that are popular today, the ones that are needlepointed, embroidered, quilted, or appliqued. Make a rather elaborate flower arrangement in a crystal or silver container (to fit in with the idea of luxury), and then pile pillows on both sides of the flower centerpiece.

Addition—One banner lettered, "At the rich man's gate, lay a beggar" and another "Woe to the complacent."

Celebration

Ask the pastor of an inner-city parish (or a parish in a poorer section of town) if some of your parishioners can be guests at one of their liturgies. Announce this in your bulletin and organize some carpools so that you can follow each other there. This will be an eye-opening experience for some people, who may not be aware of the poverty in which many of their brothers and sisters live. It could give them an entirely new outlook on their own lives.

Reflection

Today's first reading is addressed to the complacent who are stretched comfortably on their couches, eating and drinking and listening to music, unconcerned about the problems of others. Our altar decoration reminds us that, although we sometimes complain about needing to count our pennies, most of us lead a comfortable life, and have a more luxurious lifestyle than the people in the poorest parts of our own city. Take a moment each day this week to try to imagine what it would be like to live in a house with no heat, or air conditioning, or electricity, or plumbing, and little hope of moving out or up. Think how it would feel to be one of the street people, always wandering, always hungry. In the midst of our many blessings, let us not be complacent or forget the beggars who lie at our gate.

Twenty-Seventh Sunday in Ordinary Time

Habakkuk 1: 2-3; 2, 2-4
2 Timothy 1: 6-8, 13-14
Luke 17: 5-10

The Apostles said to the Lord, "Increase our faith."

Decoration
To indicate growth, use one very small plant. To the right of it, place a bit larger plant, then another still larger, and finally, a flourishing and healthy large green plant. To the left of the plants, put a watering can, garden gloves, a trowel, a weeder, pruning shears and a "how-to" book about gardening.

Addition—Two banners with the design of a vine climbing up the side, one lettered "Cultivate your faith so it may grow," another "Never be ashamed of your testimony to our Lord."

Celebration
If you have a parish study club, ask one of the representatives to give a short talk about it and invite parishioners to join. If you don't have one, make plans to organize one. Many parishes have benefitted from the "Renew" program or the "De Sales" program. Others have chosen an adult catechism book, then organized small groups to study and discuss the subjects presented in the book.

Reflection
In today's Gospel, the Apostles say to the Lord, "Increase our faith." In the second reading, we are told to "stir into flame the gift of God bestowed on you" and "never be ashamed of your testimony to our Lord." Many people take the gift of faith for granted. They study religion in grade school, and maybe in high school, and then think they know

all there is to know about God. They take refresher courses to keep current in their business or profession, exchange recipes and read cook books, take bridge lessons, or tennis lessons, or exercise classes. But they quit learning about God, the most complex subject of all. Today's altar decoration reminds us that to grow in faith, we need to cultivate it, work at it, read about it, study it, seed it and weed it.

Twenty-Eighth Sunday in Ordinary Time

2 Kings 5: 14-17
2 Timothy 2: 8-13
Luke 17: 11-19

Was there no one to return and give thanks to God except this foreigner?

Decoration
Make a large oversized thank you card for the center of the decoration, then surround it with an assortment of pretty or interesting or funny thank you cards from a card shop. Next to each card, put a snapshot of someone you could or should thank: parents, grandparents, a teacher, a coach, a priest or bishop. Intersperse items with flowers and greenery.

Addition—A mobile made with cards on which you have lettered the words "thank you" in different languages—*gracias, merci,* etc. One banner lettered "One came back praising God in a loud voice." A second banner lettered "Where are the other nine?"

Celebration
Perhaps you could go to a card shop or discount store and buy a large number of inexpensive thank you notes. Put them in baskets with bows tied on the handles and either put the baskets on the altar and invite people to come up and take one, or have someone stand at the door and hand out the thank you notes as people leave Mass. Ask that each person send one to someone who has made a difference in his or her life.

Reflection
In today's Gospel, Jesus healed ten lepers, but only one returned to say thanks and to praise God in a loud voice. We often neglect to give the gift of appreciation to each other.

Think of all the people who have made an important difference in your life, people who have helped you or healed you, cheered you, taught you, or put up with you when you were your most difficult: people like parents, grandparents, teachers, bosses, spouses, neighbors, and children. Have you said thank you to them? Have you let them know how much you appreciate their help and love? And what about your priests and pastor? What about God? Do you say a short prayer of thanks every morning for another new day? Do you say a thanksgiving before you go to sleep at night? This week, think about who you appreciate, who you've neglected, who deserves more of your thank you's.

Twenty-Ninth Sunday in Ordinary Time

Exodus 17: 8-13
2 Timothy 3: 14-4: 2
Luke 18, 1-8

I charge you to preach the word, to stay with this task whether convenient or inconvenient—correcting, reproving, appealing—constantly teaching and never losing patience.

Decoration

Again, use a Bible as the center of the decoration. This time, surround it with things that indicate the media—copies of *TV Guide*, videotape boxes, cassette tapes, a newspaper, small radio or tape player, a TV remote control. Take two fairly large bowls and anchor a fat candle in the center of each. Then fill the bowls with popcorn, so that the popcorn bowls become your candleholders (since we often eat popcorn while watching TV or videotapes). Put one bowl at each end of the display and add some greenery around the base, but no flowers (this way the popcorn will show up better).

Addition—Large banner to hang behind altar, lettered "I charge you to preach the word—whether convenient or inconvenient."

Celebration

Make a list of the names and addresses of local television and radio stations, television networks, and local newspapers. Make enough copies to put in the pews, or have them available at the doors of the church so that people can take them home.

Reflection

In today's second reading, Paul tells us to "remain faithful to what you have learned..." and reminds us that Scripture is the source of the wisdom that leads to salvation. Unfortunately, it seems that the media has become the "Bible" of many people today, as our altar decoration suggests. How often we see television programs that go against all the morals and values Scripture has taught us, and yet we do not complain or object. Paul tells us that whether it is convenient or inconvenient, we must correct, reprove, and teach, never losing patience.

It's a lot of trouble to constantly point out to our children the false values that so many TV programs teach, to constantly reprove, and correct, and never lose patience. It's a lot of trouble to write to the networks or sponsors and object to immoral TV shows, incorrect newspaper reporting, or biased news programs that present only one side of the story. And yet Paul tells us we must do this; we must remain faithful to what we have learned and believe.

Thirtieth Sunday in Ordinary Time

Sirach 35: 12-14
2 Timothy 4: 6-8, 16-18
Luke 18: 9-14

The prayer of the lowly pierces the clouds; it does not rest until it reaches its goal.

Decoration

Today's focus is on prayer. You can probably find a small statue of hands folded in prayer, or a photograph of the drawing called "The Praying Hands." Or you could use the statue that shows one large hand (God's) with a child snuggled inside it. (You should be able to find one of these statues at a Catholic or Christian book/gift store, or a ceramic shop). Elevate the statue or mounted picture in some way—sit it on a footed cake stand, or place it on a tall, inverted flower pot or vase, or use another type of pedestal. On each side place a silver or crystal bowl filled with small, folded slips of paper (like petitions). Surround the whole arrangement with greenery and lighted vigil lights.

Addition—Make a mobile with the design of white, fluffy clouds. Two banners, one lettered "I will bless the Lord at all times," and the other lettered "The Lord knows no favorites."

Celebration

Arrange to have several different people present petitions during the prayer of the faithful—a child, a teenager, a parent, a nun or teacher, a senior citizen. The petitions could be appropriate for their time of life; for example, the child might say, "Help little children to be your friends, Lord, and learn your rules for a good life, for this we pray..." or from a senior citizen "Give older people strength and patience, Lord, to accept the afflictions of age and to continue to do your work, for this we pray...."

Reflection

In today's readings, we hear that the Lord knows no favorites. He hears the cry of the poor—not only those who are financially poor but also the poor in spirit, the oppressed, the broken-hearted. Petitions reach the heavens and pierce the clouds. The prayer of the lowly does not rest until it reaches its goal.

But this prayer cannot be like that of the self-righteous man in the Gospel, who gave thanks that he was "not sinful like the rest of men." Prayer should be a sincere pouring out of self, giving God all our cares and concerns, all our praise and thanksgiving. Today's altar decoration shows vigil lights, and bowls filled with petitions that symbolize the petitions of all our parish. This is a reminder for us all to pray always, and always to pray sincerely.

Thirty-First Sunday in Ordinary Time

Wisdom 11: 22-12, 1
2 Thessalonians 1: 11—2: 2
Luke 19: 1-10

You overlook the sins of men that they may repent...you loathe nothing that you have made.

Decoration

Since you can't bring in a sycamore tree like the one Zacchaeus climbs in today's Gospel, put a ladder at each end of today's decoration, either simple, aluminum ladders or colorful, decorated stepladders. Put a copper tray on one side of the decoration itself, and pile it high with "gold" jewelry (you can find some at flea markets or garage sales or borrow some from your friends). On the other side, put a copper bowl filled with shiny oranges. Use yellow flowers like chrysanthemums for a center arrangement and a dark-colored cloth to make the gold show up brightly.

Addition—Two banners, one lettered "The Lord is kind and full of compassion," the other lettered, "Jesus came to search out and save what was lost."

Celebration

Have a "forgiving time" today after communion. Ask those present to sit in silence for a few minutes and think of anyone in their life who needs their forgiveness. Tell them to "give this to God, and ask God to help you forgive them."

Reflection

Today's readings and our altar decorations show us how God sees the true gold in the world. God sees an orange or a golden flower as valuable as gold. The Creator loathes nothing that has been made by divine ordination, and has infinite compassion for sinners so that they may be saved. The ladders remind us that Zacchaeus climbed a sycamore tree just to get a better look at Jesus. The world hated and shunned this tax collector, but Jesus saw the goodness in him and showed him special favor by going to his house.

Today Jesus has come to our house by way of the eucharist. Let us sit quietly with him for a few minutes after communion to share a "forgiving time." Ask Jesus to forgive you and to help you forgive others. Think quietly if there is someone in your life against whom you feel resentment or anger, anyone who has wronged you or hurt you, anyone who you have never been able to forgive. Offer up this resentment, anger, or hurt and ask Jesus to help you forgive as he forgives.

Thirty-Second Sunday in Ordinary Time

2 Maccabees 7: 1-2, 9-14
1 Thessalonians 5: 1-6
Luke 20: 27-38 or 20: 27, 34-38

May God who loved us and in his mercy gave us eternal consolation and hope, console your hearts and strengthen them for every good work and word.

Decoration

Letter a poster or sign "We commission you ministers of praise." Use this in the center of your decoration. (If this would be too large you could just use the words "We commission you..." or "Ministers of Praise.") Instead of flowers, try to get branches of bittersweet or pyracantha, since these have thorns but also have beautiful orange berries. On one side place a silver tray or another type of container to hold cards with each of the names of those to be commissioned. On the other side, place a tray with the awards or certificates they are to receive.

Addition—Large banner behind the altar, lettered "Console your hearts and strengthen them for every good work and word."

Celebration

Many parishes have commissioning services for the various parish minsters: lectors, eucharistic ministers, catechists, and the like. Some parishes also have a commissioning service for ministers of praise. These are the ill, the elderly, the retarded, the handicapped—generally house-bound people who spend time in prayer for special intentions. If you would like to start this in your parish, you can put a carefully-worded announcement in the bulletin several weeks ahead of time, asking for the names of possible ministers. Then plan to have a commissioning ceremony. Contact the "caretakers" well in advance so that they can make arrangements to be at the church for Mass that day. The service itself should be brief. Have appropriate music as the ministers gather in front of the altar. One altar person could hold the tray with names, another the tray with the awards. Choose awards that are tangible, like a Jerusalem cross, a crucifix, or a large medal. The priest could use the first lines from today's second reading, and add a simple prayer that "through your suffering and prayers, you will serve as a minister of praise for this parish."

Reflection

Today's readings speak of courage. The first tells of the brothers who suffered bravely for God's sake, while the second prays that God will strengthen us for good works and words. The Gospel reminds us that "all are alive for God." In keeping with these readings, our altar is decorated for today's special commissioning service where our parish will commission some very brave and courageous people to act as our ministers of praise.

Thirty-Third Sunday in Ordinary Time

Malachi 3: 19-20
2 Thessalonians 3: 7-12
Luke 21: 5-19

There will arise the sun of justice with its healing rays.

Decoration
Take strips of varicolored felt or posterboard. Glue them to a backdrop of fabric or posterboard in such a way as to create a sunburst effect, one of rays going out. At the center of the rays put a globe to illustrate our world receiving the healing rays. Flank this with greenery and flowers.

Addition—A banner lettered "There will arise the sun of justice with its healing rays." A second banner designed with colored rays. At the center of the rays, put a white circle (like a host) overlaid with a black or brown cross. At the bottom of the banner, put the word "Alleluia."

Celebration
Go to an instant print shop and have them print some cards—about the size of a holy card—that read: "If you were on trial for being a Christian, would there be enough evidence to convict you?" Distribute a card to all parishioners as they leave Mass.

Reflection
Today's readings make us think of the "now" and the "not yet." They speak of the temple being destroyed, and of the day coming when all evildoers will be stubble. But as always, there is a promise. Our altar decorations reflect the words of the first reading which promises us that after the destruction, "there will arise the sun of justice with its healing rays."

This week, think about how well you are prepared for the time to come. Is your "now" the kind of life that will help you be prepared for the "not yet?" If you are judged justly, will you be one who receives the healing rays? Think about the question, "If you were on trial for being a Christian, would there be enough evidence to convict you?"

Christ the King

2 Samuel 5: 1-3
Colossians 1: 12-20
Luke 23: 35-43

There was this inscription over his head, "This is the king of the Jews."

Decoration

Since this feast falls in harvest time, near Thanksgiving, use a large cornucopia at each end of the altar, spilling forth fresh vegetables and fruit, gourds, and colorful squash. Add fall flowers, autumn leaves, seed pods, nuts—anything to indicate the riches of harvest time. In the center of the arrangement, put a few tall dried flowers, cattails, or stalks of wheat and center this with a tall golden cross. In front of the cross, have a large satin pillow with a crown on it. Make the crown of foil, sequins, and "jewels" from some old costume jewelry. Or you might be able to rent a crown from a costume shop. Just be sure that the crown is appropriately elaborate for this feast of the King! If the final arrangement looks too busy, just use the center arrangement and put two large candles in golden candle holders on each side.

Addition—A mobile with several different designs of crowns. A banner with the crown design, lettered "Blessed is the one who inherits the kingdom." Another with the design of the cross, lettered "This day you will be with me in paradise."

Celebration

Purchase four of the many "windsocks" designed to flutter on a patio or porch, and attach them to long poles or dowel rods. Have four children lead the entrance procession, carrying these as though they are the king's flags. If possible, have bases positioned so the children can stand the flags at each of the four corners of the altar. If not, they could hang them on hooks on the rear wall behind the altar. Possibly have a fifth child walk behind them, carrying the satin pillow with the crown on it that will then be placed at the center of today's decoration.

Reflection

Today, in the midst of harvest time, we celebrate the feast of Christ the King, the savior who has earned for us a chance to share in the rich harvest of heaven. Jesus was a king, but he reigned from a cross rather than a throne. Because of him, today's Christians can see the glory in the cross and the value of pain or suffering when it leads to the reward of the crown. Let us rejoice today that we are heirs to the kingdom, that we have been invited to the house of the Lord.